Working Papers

for use with

Prepared by SHEILA F. ELWORTHY
CA SCHOOL OF BUSINESS

and TANA M. KRISTJANSON
CAMOSUN COLLEGE

NELSON / EDUCATION

NELSON EDUCATION

Working Papers
by Sheila F. Elworthy and
Tana M. Kristjanson

**for use with *Accounting,* Volume 1,
Second Canadian Edition**
by Carl S. Warren, James M. Reeve,
Jonathan E. Duchac, Sheila F. Elworthy,
Tana M. Kristjanson, and Barrie E. Tober

**Vice President, Editorial
Higher Education:**
Anne Williams

Senior Acquisitions Editor:
Amie Plourde

Marketing Manager:
David Stratton

Developmental Editor:
Lisa Berland

**Senior Content Production
Manager:**
Imoinda Romain

Manufacturing Manager:
Joanne McNeil

Design Director:
Ken Phipps

Managing Designer:
Franca Amore

Cover Design:
Liz Harasymczuk

Cover Image:
Scott Gilchrist/Masterfile

Contents

Volume 1

Preface

The working papers include problem-specific forms for preparing solutions for Exercises, Problems, the Continuing Problem, and the Comprehensive Problems from the textbook. These forms, with preprinted headings, provide a structure for the problems, which will help you get started and save you time.

The authors would like to thank Paul B. Elworthy, MBA, for his accuracy check of these working papers.

EXERCISE 1-1

a.

1. _____   5. _____   9. _____
2. _____   6. _____   10. _____
3. _____   7. _____   11. _____
4. _____   8. _____   12. _____

b. _____
_____

EXERCISE 1-2

1. _____   6. _____
2. _____   7. _____
3. _____   8. _____
4. _____   9. _____
5. _____

EXERCISE 1-3

a. _____
_____
_____

b. _____
_____
_____

EXERCISE 1-4

Principle Violated	Correction
_____	_____
_____	_____
_____	_____
_____	_____
_____	_____
_____	_____
_____	_____
_____	_____
_____	_____
_____	_____
_____	_____
_____	_____

EXERCISE 1-4, Continued

_____   _____
_____   _____
_____   _____
_____   _____
_____   _____
_____   _____
_____   _____
_____   _____
_____   _____
_____   _____
_____   _____
_____   _____
_____   _____
_____   _____
_____   _____
_____   _____

EXERCISE 1-5

1. _____
2. _____
3. _____
4. _____
5. _____
6. _____

EXERCISE 1-6

1. _____
2. _____
3. _____
4. _____
5. _____
6. _____

EXERCISE 1-7

	Assets	=	**Liabilities**	+	**Owner's Equity**
a.	_____	=	$250,000	+	$780,000
b.	$125,000	=	_____	+	39,500
c.	60,000	=	7,500	+	_____

EXERCISE 1-8

a. _____

b. _____

c. _____

d. _____

e. _____

EXERCISE 1-9

a. Accounts payable: _____

b. Cash: _____

c. Fees earned: _____

d. Accounts receivable _____

e. Land: _____

f. Supplies: _____

g. Wages expense: _____

h. Mark Flinn, Withdrawals: _____

EXERCISE 1-10

a. _____

b. _____

c. _____

d. _____

e. _____

EXERCISE 1-11

a. **1.** Assets:_____

   2. Liabilities:_____

   3. Owner's equity:_____

b. **1.** Assets:_____

   2. Liabilities:_____

   3. Owner's equity:_____

c. _____

_____

_____

_____

_____

EXERCISE 1-12

1. Expenses: _____

2. Revenues: _____

3. Owner's investments: _____

4. Owner's withdrawals: _____

EXERCISE 1-13

1. _____   6. _____

2. _____   7. _____

3. _____   8. _____

4. _____   9. _____

5. _____

EXERCISE 1-14

a. (1) _____

   (2) _____

   (3) _____

   (4) _____

   (5) _____

   (6) _____

b. _____

c. _____

d. _____

e. _____

EXERCISE 1-15

_____

_____

_____

_____

_____

_____

_____

EXERCISE 1-16

Aries:	
Gemini:	
Leo:	
Pisces:	

EXERCISE 1-17

1. Accounts Payable: _____
2. Cash: _____
3. Fees Earned: _____
4. Land: _____
5. Sarah Neil, Capital: _____
6. Supplies: _____
7. Supplies Expense: _____
8. Utilities Expense: _____
9. Wages Expense: _____
10. Wages Payable: _____

EXERCISE 1-18

1. Accounts Payable: _____
2. Cash: _____
3. Fees Earned: _____
4. Land: _____
5. Sarah Neil, Capital: _____
6. Supplies: _____
7. Supplies Expense: _____
8. Utilities Expense: _____
9. Wages Expense: _____
10. Wages Payable: _____

EXERCISE 1-19

a. _____

Statement of Owner's Equity

b. _____

EXERCISE 1-20

	Income Statement		

EXERCISE 1-21

Aquarius:		
Libra:		
Scorpio:		
Taurus:		

EXERCISE 1-22

a.

	Balance Sheet		

	Balance Sheet		

b.

c.

EXERCISE 1-23

a. **(1)**Accounts payable and accrued liabilities:_____

    (2) Cash and cash equivalents:_____

    (3) Operating expenses:_____

    (4) Income taxes payable:_____

    (5) Revenues, net of royalties:_____

    (6) Long-term debt:_____

    (7) Other liabilities and provisions:_____

    (8) Property, plant and equipment, net:_____

    (9) Investments and other assets:_____

    (10) Transportation expenses:_____

b. _____

_____

_____

PROBLEM 1-1 _____

1.

	ASSETS			=	LIABILITIES	+	OWNER'S EQUITY						
	Cash	+	Accounts Receivable	+	Supplies	=	Accounts Payable	+	Capital	−	With-drawals	+	Fees Earned	−	Rent Exp.	−	Sal. Exp.	−	Auto Exp.	−	Misc. Exp.
a.														
b.														
c.														
d.														
e.														
f.														
g.														
h.														
i.														
Bal.														

2.

3.

4.

This page not used.

PROBLEM 1-2___

1.

	ASSETS			=	LIABILITIES	+	OWNER'S EQUITY							
	Cash	+	Accounts Receivable	+	Supplies	=	Accounts Payable	+	Capital	−	With-drawals	+	Fees Earned	−	Rent Exp.	−	Sal. Exp.	−	Auto Exp.	−	Misc. Exp.
a.															
b.															
c.															
d.															
e.															
f.															
g.															
h.															
i.															
Bal.															

2.

This page not used.

PROBLEM 1-3___

1.

Income Statement		

2.

Statement of Owner's Equity		

PROBLEM 1-3 ___ , Concluded

3.

Balance Sheet			

PROBLEM 1-4___

1.

	Income Statement		

2.

	Statement of Owner's Equity		

PROBLEM 1-4 ___ , Concluded

3.

	Balance Sheet			

PROBLEM 1-5 ___

1.

	ASSETS		=	LIABILITIES	+	OWNER'S EQUITY							
	Cash	+	Supplies	=	Accounts Payable	+	Capital	– Withdrawals +	Sales Comm.	– Office Sal. Exp.	– Rent Exp. –	Auto Exp.	– Misc. Exp.
a.													
b.													
c.													
d.													
e.													
f.													
g.													
h.													
Bal.													

PROBLEM 1-5 ___ , Continued

2.

	Income Statement		

	Statement of Owner's Equity		

PROBLEM 1-5 ___, Concluded

2.

	Balance Sheet			

This page not used.

PROBLEM 1-6 _____

1.

		ASSETS					LIABILITIES		OWNER'S EQUITY
Cash	+	Accounts Receivable	+	Supplies	+	Land	=	Accounts Payable	+	____,Capital
	+		+		+		=		+	____, Capital
	+		+		+		=		+	____, Capital
							=		+	____, Capital
							=		+	____, Capital

PROBLEM 1-6 ____, Continued

2.

	ASSETS				= LIABILITIES +	OWNER'S EQUITY								
		Accts.				Accts.				Dry Cleaning	Dry Cleaning	Wages	Rent	Truck		Misc.
	Cash +	Rec. +	Supplies +	Land =		Pay. +	Capital -	Withdrawals +	Revenue -	Exp. -	Exp. -	Exp. -	Exp. -	Exp. -	Util. Exp.-	Exp.
Bal.																
a.																
b.																
c.																
d.																
e.																
f.																
g.																
h.																
i.																
j.																
k.																
Bal.																

PROBLEM 1-6___ , Continued

3.

Income Statement

Statement of Owner's Equity

PROBLEM 1-6___ , Concluded

3.

Balance Sheet				

PROBLEM 1-7___

1.   a._____

_____

b._____

_____

c._____

_____

d._____

_____

e._____

_____

f._____

_____

g._____

_____

h._____

_____

i._____

_____

2.

Income Statement

PROBLEM 1-7 ___ , Concluded

Statement of Owner's Equity			

3.

Balance Sheet			

PROBLEM 1-8 ___

1. a. _____
_____

b. _____
_____

c. _____
_____

d. _____
_____

e. _____
_____

f. _____
_____

g. _____
_____

h. _____
_____

i. _____
_____

j. _____
_____

This page not used.

CONTINUING PROBLEM

1.

	ASSETS			= LIABILITIES +	OWNER'S EQUITY					
	Cash +	Accts. Rec. +	Supplies =	Accts. Pay. +	Pat Sharpe, Capital +	Pat Sharpe, With- drawals −	Fees Earned +	−	Music Exp.	− Adv. Exp.
11/1										
11/2										
11/2										
11/4										
11/6										
11/13										
11/22										
11/29										
Bal.										
11/30										
Bal.										

CONTINUING PROBLEM, Continued

1.

	ASSETS			= LIABILITIES	+		OWNER'S EQUITY								
Cash +	Accts. Rec. +	Supplies =		Accts. Pay.		Lee Chang, + Capital –	Lee Chang,W ith- drawals +	Fees Earned –	Music Exp. –	Office Rent Exp. –	Equip. Rent Exp. –	Adv. Exp. –	Wages Exp. –	Util. Exp. –	Misc. Exp.
Bal.															
11/30															
Bal.															
11/30															
Bal.															
11/30															
Bal.															
11/30															
Bal.															
11/30															
Bal.															

CONTINUING PROBLEM, Continued

2.

Income Statement			

3.

Statement of Owner's Equity			

CONTINUING PROBLEM, Concluded

4.

Balance Sheet			

EXERCISE 2-1

Accounts Payable and Accrued Liabilities: _____

Aeroplan Miles Obligation: _____

Aircraft Fuel Expenses: _____

Cargo Revenue: _____

Commissions: _____

Property and Equipment: _____

Airport and Navigation Fees: _____

Passenger Revenue: _____

Deposits and Other Assets: _____

Spare Parts, Materials, and Supplies: _____

EXERCISE 2-2

Account	Account Number
Accounts Payable	_____
Accounts Receivable..............	_____
Cash......................................	_____
Fees Earned...........................	_____
Land	_____
Miscellaneous Expense	_____
Tony Newbaurer, Capital	_____
Tony Newbaurer, Withdrawals	_____
Wages Expense.....................	_____

EXERCISE 2-3

Balance Sheet Accounts

Acct #	Account Name
	1. Assets
	2. Liabilities
	3. Owner's Equity

Income Statement Accounts

Acct #	Account Name
	4. Revenue
	5. Expenses

EXERCISE 2-4

a. and b.

Transaction	Account Debited – Type	Account Debited – Effect	Account Credited – Type	Account Credited – Effect
(1)	asset	+	owner's equity	+
(2)				
(3)				
(4)				
(5)				
(6)				
(7)				
(8)				

EXERCISE 2-5

JOURNAL   PAGE _____

	DATE		DESCRIPTION	POST. REF.	DEBIT	CREDIT	
1							1
2							2
3							3
4							4
5							5
6							6
7							7
8							8
9							9
10							10
11							11
12							12
13							13
14							14
15							15
16							16
17							17
18							18
19							19
20							20
21							21

EXERCISE 2-5, Concluded

JOURNAL   PAGE

	DATE		DESCRIPTION	POST. REF.	DEBIT	CREDIT	
1							1
2							2
3							3
4							4
5							5
6							6
7							7
8							8

EXERCISE 2-6

Unadjusted Trial Balance

EXERCISE 2-7

1. Accounts Payable: _____

2. Accounts Receivable: _____

3. Cash: _____

4. Fees Earned: _____

5. Insurance Expense: _____

6. Nick Swanson, Withdrawals: _____

EXERCISE 2-8

a. Accounts Payable: _____

b. Accounts Receivable: _____

c. Barbara Mallary, Capital: _____

d. Barbara Mallary, Withdrawals: _____

e. Cash: _____

f. Fees Earned: _____

g. Office Equipment: _____

h. Rent Expense: _____

i. Supplies: _____

j. Wages Expense: _____

EXERCISE 2-9

	Increase	Decrease	Normal Balance
Balance sheet accounts:			
Asset....................................	Debit	**(a)** _____	**(b)** _____
Liability..................................	Credit	**(c)** _____	**(d)** _____
Owner's Equity:			
Capital	**(e)** _____	Debit	**(f)** _____
Withdrawals...................	**(g)** _____	**(h)** _____	Debit
Income statement accounts:			
Revenue	**(i)** _____	**(j)** _____	**(k)** _____
Expense..............................	**(l)** _____	Credit	Debit

EXERCISE 2-10

_____

_____

_____

_____

_____

EXERCISE 2-11

a. _____

_____

_____

b. _____

EXERCISE 2-12

a.

Accounts Payable

b.

Accounts Receivable

c.

Cash

EXERCISE 2-13

JOURNAL

	DATE		DESCRIPTION	POST. REF.	DEBIT	CREDIT	
1							1
2							2
3							3
4							4
5							5
6							6
7							7
8							8
9							9
10							10
11							11
12							12
13							13
14							14
15							15
16							16
17							17
18							18
19							19
20							20
21							21
22							22
23							23
24							24
25							25
26							26
27							27
28							28
29							29
30							30
31							31
32							32

EXERCISE 2-14

a.

<center>**JOURNAL**</center>					PAGE

	DATE		DESCRIPTION	POST. REF.	DEBIT	CREDIT	
1							1
2							2
3							3
4							4
5							5
6							6
7							7

b., c., d.

ACCOUNT						ACCOUNT NO.	

DATE		ITEM	POST. REF.	DEBIT	CREDIT	BALANCE	

ACCOUNT						ACCOUNT NO.	

DATE		ITEM	POST. REF.	DEBIT	CREDIT	BALANCE	

EXERCISE 2-15

a.

JOURNAL   PAGE

	DATE	DESCRIPTION	POST. REF.	DEBIT	CREDIT	
1						1
2						2
3						3
4						4
5						5
6						6
7						7
8						8
9						9
10						10
11						11

b.

Cash   *Accounts Payable*

Supplies   *Fees Earned*

Accounts Receivable

EXERCISE 2-16

	Unadjusted Trial Balance		

EXERCISE 2-17

EXERCISE 2-18

Unadjusted Trial Balance

EXERCISE 2-19

Error	(a) Out of Balance	(b) Difference	(c) Larger Total
1.	yes	$6,150	debit
2.			
3.			
4.			
5.			
6.			
7.			

EXERCISE 2-20

1. _____

2. _____

3. _____

4. _____

5. _____

6. _____

7. _____

_____

(Optional)

_____

Unadjusted Trial Balance

EXERCISE 2-21

1.   **JOURNAL**   PAGE

	DATE		DESCRIPTION	POST. REF.	DEBIT	CREDIT	
1							1
2							2
3							3
4							4
5							5
6							
7							

2. a.   **JOURNAL**   PAGE

	DATE		DESCRIPTION	POST. REF.	DEBIT	CREDIT	
1							1
2							2
3							3
4							4
5							5
6							
7							

2. b.

_____

_____

_____

_____

_____

EXERCISE 2-22

a.   **JOURNAL**   PAGE

	DATE		DESCRIPTION	POST. REF.	DEBIT	CREDIT	
1							1
2							2
3							3
4							4
5							5
6							
7							

b.   **JOURNAL**   PAGE

	DATE		DESCRIPTION	POST. REF.	DEBIT	CREDIT	
1							1
2							2
3							3
4							4
5							5
6							
7							

This page not used

PROBLEM 2-1 ___

Cash

Accounts Receivable

_____ , *Capital*

_____ , *Withdrawals*

Advertising Expense

Miscellaneous Expense

Fees Earned

PROBLEM 2-1 ___, Concluded

Telephone Expense

PROBLEM 2-2 ___

1. and 2.

Cash

Accounts Receivable

Supplies

Equipment

PROBLEM 2-2 ___, Continued

Accounts Payable

_____, Capital

Professional Fees

Rent Expense

Blueprint Expense

Miscellaneous Expense

PROBLEM 2-2 ___ , Concluded

3.

Unadjusted Trial Balance		

This page not used

PROBLEM 2-3 ___

1. and 2.

Cash

Prepaid Insurance

Automobiles

Equipment

Accounts Payable

Note Payable

PROBLEM 2-3 ___, Concluded

_____, *Capital*

Salary Expense

Automobile Expense

3.

_____

Unadjusted Trial Balance

PROBLEM 2-4 ___

1.

	DATE	**DESCRIPTION**	**POST. REF.**	**DEBIT**	**CREDIT**
1					
2					
3					
4					
5					
6					
7					
8					
9					
10					
11					
12					
13					
14					
15					
16					
17					
18					
19					
20					
21					
22					
23					
24					
25					
26					
27					
28					
29					
30					
31					
32					
33					
34					
35					
36					

JOURNAL   PAGE

PROBLEM 2-4 ___, Continued

2.

Cash

Supplies

Accounts Payable

_____, *Capital*

_____, *Withdrawals*

Sales Commissions

PROBLEM 2-4 ___, Continued

Rent Expense

Office Salaries Expense

Automobile Expense

Miscellaneous Expense

PROBLEM 2-4 ___, Concluded

3.

	Unadjusted Trial Balance	

4. a. _____

    b. _____

    c. _____

PROBLEM 2-5 ___

1.

		JOURNAL					PAGE *1*

	DATE		DESCRIPTION	POST. REF.	DEBIT	CREDIT	
1							1
2							2
3							3
4							4
5							5
6							6
7							7
8							8
9							9
10							10
11							11
12							12
13							13
14							14
15							15

PROBLEM 2-5 ___, Continued

JOURNAL   PAGE 2

	DATE		DESCRIPTION	POST. REF.	DEBIT	CREDIT	
1							1
2							2
3							3
4							4
5							5
6							6
7							7
8							8
9							9
10							10
11							11
12							12

PROBLEM 2-5 ___ , Continued

2.

GENERAL LEDGER

ACCOUNT   *Cash*   ACCOUNT NO.   *1010*

DATE		ITEM	POST. REF.	DEBIT	CREDIT	BALANCE
		12				

ACCOUNT   *Accounts Receivable*   ACCOUNT NO.   *1020*

DATE		ITEM	POST. REF.	DEBIT	CREDIT	BALANCE

ACCOUNT   *Supplies*   ACCOUNT NO.   *1030*

DATE		ITEM	POST. REF.	DEBIT	CREDIT	BALANCE

ACCOUNT   *Equipment*   ACCOUNT NO.   *1060*

DATE		ITEM	POST. REF.	DEBIT	CREDIT	BALANCE

PROBLEM 2-5 ___, Continued

ACCOUNT   *Accounts Payable*   ACCOUNT NO.   *2020*

DATE		ITEM	POST. REF.	DEBIT	CREDIT	BALANCE

ACCOUNT   _____, *Capital*   ACCOUNT NO.   *3010*

DATE		ITEM	POST. REF.	DEBIT	CREDIT	BALANCE

ACCOUNT   _____, *Withdrawals*   ACCOUNT NO.   *3020*

DATE		ITEM	POST. REF.	DEBIT	CREDIT	BALANCE

ACCOUNT   *Fees Earned*   ACCOUNT NO.   *4010*

DATE		ITEM	POST. REF.	DEBIT	CREDIT	BALANCE

ACCOUNT   *Rent Expense*   ACCOUNT NO.   *5030*

DATE		ITEM	POST. REF.	DEBIT	CREDIT	BALANCE

PROBLEM 2-5 ___, Continued

ACCOUNT   *Utilities Expense*   ACCOUNT NO.   *5040*

DATE		ITEM	POST. REF.	DEBIT	CREDIT	BALANCE

PROBLEM 2-5 ___, Concluded

3.

Unadjusted Trial Balance		

PROBLEM 2-6 ___

1.

JOURNAL

PAGE *1*

	DATE		DESCRIPTION	POST. REF.	DEBIT	CREDIT	
1							1
2							2
3							3
4							4
5							5
6							6
7							7
8							8
9							9
10							10
11							11
12							12
13							13
14							14
15							15

PROBLEM 2-6 ___, Continued

| | | JOURNAL | | | PAGE 2 |

	DATE	DESCRIPTION	POST. REF.	DEBIT	CREDIT	
1						1
2						2
3						3
4						4
5						5
6						6
7						7
8						8
9						9
10						10
11						11
12						12

PROBLEM 2-6 ___, Continued

2.

GENERAL LEDGER

ACCOUNT *Cash*   ACCOUNT NO. *1010*

DATE		ITEM	POST. REF.	DEBIT	CREDIT	BALANCE
		12				

ACCOUNT *Accounts Receivable*   ACCOUNT NO. *1020*

DATE		ITEM	POST. REF.	DEBIT	CREDIT	BALANCE

ACCOUNT *Prepaid Insurance Account*   ACCOUNT NO. *1050*

DATE		ITEM	POST. REF.	DEBIT	CREDIT	BALANCE

ACCOUNT *Unearned Deposit*   ACCOUNT NO. *2020*

DATE		ITEM	POST. REF.	DEBIT	CREDIT	BALANCE

PROBLEM 2-6 ___, Continued

ACCOUNT   *Loan Payable*   ACCOUNT NO.   *2030*

DATE		ITEM	POST. REF.	DEBIT	CREDIT	BALANCE

ACCOUNT   _____, *Capital*   ACCOUNT NO.   *3010*

DATE		ITEM	POST. REF.	DEBIT	CREDIT	BALANCE

ACCOUNT   *Fees Earned*   ACCOUNT NO.   *4010*

DATE		ITEM	POST. REF.	DEBIT	CREDIT	BALANCE

ACCOUNT   *Wages Expense*   ACCOUNT NO.   *5010*

DATE		ITEM	POST. REF.	DEBIT	CREDIT	BALANCE

ACCOUNT   *Miscellaneous Expense*   ACCOUNT NO.   *5090*

DATE		ITEM	POST. REF.	DEBIT	CREDIT	BALANCE

PROBLEM 2-6 ___, Concluded

3.

Unadjusted Trial Balance

This page not used

PROBLEM 2-7 ___

2.

JOURNAL

PAGE *18*

	DATE		DESCRIPTION	POST. REF.	DEBIT	CREDIT	
1							1
2							2
3							3
4							4
5							5
6							6
7							7
8							8
9							9
10							10
11							11
12							12
13							13
14							14
15							15
16							16
17							17
18							18
19							19
20							20
21							21
22							22
23							23
24							24
25							25
26							26
27							27
28							28
29							29
30							30
31							31
32							32
33							33
34							34
35							35
36							36

PROBLEM 2-7 ___, Continued

1. and 3.

GENERAL LEDGER

ACCOUNT   *Cash*   ACCOUNT NO.   *1010*

DATE		ITEM	POST. REF.	DEBIT	CREDIT	BALANCE	

ACCOUNT   *Accounts Receivable*   ACCOUNT NO.   *1020*

DATE		ITEM	POST. REF.	DEBIT	CREDIT	BALANCE	

ACCOUNT   *Office Supplies*   ACCOUNT NO.   *1040*

DATE		ITEM	POST. REF.	DEBIT	CREDIT	BALANCE	

PROBLEM 2-7 ___ , Continued

ACCOUNT   *Land*   ACCOUNT NO.   *1060*

DATE	ITEM	POST. REF.	DEBIT	CREDIT	BALANCE

ACCOUNT   *Accounts Payable*   ACCOUNT NO.   *2010*

DATE	ITEM	POST. REF.	DEBIT	CREDIT	BALANCE

ACCOUNT   *Notes Payable*   ACCOUNT NO.   *2030*

DATE	ITEM	POST. REF.	DEBIT	CREDIT	BALANCE

ACCOUNT   _____,*Capital*   ACCOUNT NO.   *3010*

DATE	ITEM	POST. REF.	DEBIT	CREDIT	BALANCE

ACCOUNT   _____,*Withdrawals*   ACCOUNT NO.   *3020*

DATE	ITEM	POST. REF.	DEBIT	CREDIT	BALANCE

PROBLEM 2-7 ___ , Continued

ACCOUNT　　*Fees Earned*　　　　　　　　　　　　　　　　ACCOUNT NO.　*4010*

DATE		ITEM	POST. REF.	DEBIT	CREDIT	BALANCE

ACCOUNT　　*Salaries and Commissions Expense*　　　　　ACCOUNT NO.　*5010*

DATE		ITEM	POST. REF.	DEBIT	CREDIT	BALANCE

ACCOUNT　　*Rent Expense*　　　　　　　　　　　　　　　ACCOUNT NO.　*5020*

DATE		ITEM	POST. REF.	DEBIT	CREDIT	BALANCE

ACCOUNT　　*Advertising Expense*　　　　　　　　　　　ACCOUNT NO.　*5030*

DATE		ITEM	POST. REF.	DEBIT	CREDIT	BALANCE

PROBLEM 2-7___, Concluded

4.

	Unadjusted Trial Balance	

This page not used

PROBLEM 2-8 ___

2.

<table>
<tr><td colspan="7" align="center">JOURNAL</td><td align="right">PAGE 18</td></tr>
<tr>
<th colspan="2">DATE</th>
<th>DESCRIPTION</th>
<th>POST.
REF.</th>
<th>DEBIT</th>
<th>CREDIT</th>
</tr>
<tr><td></td><td></td><td></td><td></td><td></td><td></td></tr>
</table>

	DATE		DESCRIPTION	POST. REF.	DEBIT	CREDIT	
1							1
2							2
3							3
4							4
5							5
6							6
7							7
8							8
9							9
10							10
11							11
12							12
13							13
14							14
15							15
16							16
17							17
18							18
19							19
20							20
21							21
22							22
23							23
24							24
25							25
26							26
27							27
28							28
29							29
30							30
31							31
32							32
33							33
34							34
35							35
36							36

PROBLEM 2-8 ___ , Continued

1. and 3.

GENERAL LEDGER

ACCOUNT   *Cash*   ACCOUNT NO.   *1010*

DATE		ITEM	POST. REF.	DEBIT	CREDIT	BALANCE

ACCOUNT   *Accounts Receivable*   ACCOUNT NO.   *1020*

DATE		ITEM	POST. REF.	DEBIT	CREDIT	BALANCE

ACCOUNT   *Prepaid Insurance Account*   ACCOUNT NO.   *1030*

DATE		ITEM	POST. REF.	DEBIT	CREDIT	BALANCE

ACCOUNT   *Sewing Supplies*   ACCOUNT NO.   *1040*

DATE		ITEM	POST. REF.	DEBIT	CREDIT	BALANCE

PROBLEM 2-8 ___, Continued

ACCOUNT   *Accounts Payable*   ACCOUNT NO.   *2010*

DATE	ITEM	POST. REF.	DEBIT	CREDIT	BALANCE

ACCOUNT   *Unearned Revenue*   ACCOUNT NO.   *2020*

DATE	ITEM	POST. REF.	DEBIT	CREDIT	BALANCE

ACCOUNT   _____*,Capital*   ACCOUNT NO.   *3010*

DATE	ITEM	POST. REF.	DEBIT	CREDIT	BALANCE

ACCOUNT   _____*,Withdrawals*   ACCOUNT NO.   *3020*

DATE	ITEM	POST. REF.	DEBIT	CREDIT	BALANCE

PROBLEM 2-8 ___, Continued

ACCOUNT   *Fees Earned*   ACCOUNT NO.   *4010*

DATE		ITEM	POST. REF.	DEBIT	CREDIT	BALANCE

ACCOUNT   *Piecework Expense*   ACCOUNT NO.   *5010*

DATE		ITEM	POST. REF.	DEBIT	CREDIT	BALANCE

ACCOUNT   *Rent Expense*   ACCOUNT NO.   *5020*

DATE		ITEM	POST. REF.	DEBIT	CREDIT	BALANCE

ACCOUNT   *Automobile Expense*   ACCOUNT NO.   *5040*

DATE		ITEM	POST. REF.	DEBIT	CREDIT	BALANCE

ACCOUNT   *Miscellaneous Expense*   ACCOUNT NO.   *5090*

DATE		ITEM	POST. REF.	DEBIT	CREDIT	BALANCE

PROBLEM 2-8 ___, Concluded

4.

	Unadjusted Trial Balance		

This page not used.

PROBLEM 2-9 ___

JOURNAL

	DATE		DESCRIPTION	POST. REF.	DEBIT	CREDIT	
1	20— May	1	Rent Expense	5020	1,540.00		1
2			Cash	1010		1,540.00	2
3							3
4		4	Supplies	1020	149.00		4
5			Accounts Payable	2020		149.00	5
6							6
7		6	Advertising Expense	5040	275.00		7
8			Cash	1010		275.00	8
9							9
10		8	Cash	1010	1,595.30		10
11			Service Revenue	4010		1,595.30	11
12							12
16		10	Land	1060	12,000.00		16
17			Cash	1010		5,500.00	17
18			Notes Payable	2010		6,500.00	18
19							19
20		13	Accounts Payable	2020	847.20		20
21			Cash	1010		847.20	21
22							22
23		14	Miscellaneous Expense	5080	162.10		23
24			Cash	1010		162.10	24
25							25
26		15	Wages Expense	5010	1,128.60		26
27			Cash	1010		1,128.60	27
28							28
29		15	Cash	1010	1,785.50		29
30			Service Revenue	4010		1,785.50	30
31							31
32		16	Tina Reid, Withdrawals	3020	750.00		32
33			Cash	1010		750.00	33
34							34
35		17	Supplies	1020	212.60		35
36			Accounts Payable	2020		212.60	36

PROBLEM 2-9 ___, Continued

JOURNAL

	DATE		DESCRIPTION	POST. REF.	DEBIT	CREDIT	
1	20— May	20	Cash	1010	1,662.20		1
2			Service Revenue	4010		1,662.20	2
3							3
4		22	Accounts Payable	2020	74.20		4
5			Supplies	1020		74.20	5
6							6
7		25	Miscellaneous Expense	5080	121.40		7
8			Cash	1010		121.40	8
9							9
10		25	Cash	1010	1,681.30		10
11			Service Revenue	4010		1,681.30	11
12							12
13		30	Utilities Expense	5030	436.60		13
14			Cash	1010		436.60	14
15							15
16		31	Wages Expense	5010	1,390.00		16
17			Cash	1010		1,390.00	17
18							18
19		31	Tina Reid, Withdrawals	3020	600.00		19
20			Cash	1010		600.00	20
21							21
22		31	Cash	1010	1,276.10		22
23			Service Revenue	4010		1,276.10	23
24							24
25							25
26							26
27							27
28							28
29							29
30							30
31							31
32							32
33							33
34							34
35							35
36							36

PROBLEM 2-9 ___ , Continued

1. and 3.

GENERAL LEDGER

ACCOUNT   *Cash*   ACCOUNT NO.   *1010*

DATE		ITEM	POST. REF.	DEBIT	CREDIT	BALANCE
20— May	1	Balance	√			13,810.00 Dr.
	1		19		1,540.00	
	6		19		275.00	
	8		19	1,595.30		
	10		19		5,500.00	
	13		19		847.20	
	14		19		162.10	
	15		19		1,128.60	
	15		19	1,785.50		
	16		19		750.00	
	20		20	1,662.20		
	25		20		121.40	
	25		20	1,681.30		
	30		20		346.60	
	31		20		1,390.00	
	31		20		600.00	
	31		20	1,276.10		9,150.00 Dr.

ACCOUNT   *Supplies*   ACCOUNT NO.   *1020*

DATE		ITEM	POST. REF.	DEBIT	CREDIT	BALANCE
20— May	1	Balance	√			710.50 Dr.
	4		19	149.00		
	17		19	212.60		
	22		20		74.20	997.90 Dr.

PROBLEM 2-9 ___ , Continued

ACCOUNT   *Land*   ACCOUNT NO.   *1060*

DATE		ITEM	POST. REF.	DEBIT	CREDIT	BALANCE
20— May	1	Balance	√	14,625.00		14,625.00 Dr.
	10		19	1,200.00		15,825.00 Dr.

ACCOUNT   *Notes Payable*   ACCOUNT NO.   *2010*

DATE		ITEM	POST. REF.	DEBIT	CREDIT	BALANCE
20— May	10		19		6,500.00	6,500.00 Cr.

ACCOUNT   *Accounts Payable*   ACCOUNT NO.   *2020*

DATE		ITEM	POST. REF.	DEBIT	CREDIT	BALANCE
20— May	1	Balance	√			1,637.30 Cr.
	4		19		149.00	
	13		19	847.20		
	17		19		212.60	
	22		20	74.20		1,151.70 CR.

ACCOUNT   *Tina Reid, Capital*   ACCOUNT NO.   *3010*

DATE		ITEM	POST. REF.	DEBIT	CREDIT	BALANCE
20— May	1	Balance	√			27,508.70 Cr.

PROBLEM 2-9 ___, Continued

ACCOUNT   *Tina Reid, Withdrawals*   ACCOUNT NO.   3020

DATE		ITEM	POST. REF.	DEBIT	CREDIT	BALANCE
20— May	16		19	750.00		
	31		20	600.00		1,350.00 Dr.

ACCOUNT   *Service Revenue*   ACCOUNT NO.   4010

DATE		ITEM	POST. REF.	DEBIT	CREDIT	BALANCE
20— May	8		19		1,595.30	
	15		19		1,785.50	
	20		20		1,662.20	
	25		20		1,681.30	
	31		20		1,276.10	8,000.40 Cr.

ACCOUNT   *Wages Expense*   ACCOUNT NO.   5010

DATE		ITEM	POST. REF.	DEBIT	CREDIT	BALANCE
20— May	15		19	1,128.60		
	31		20	1,930.00		3,058.60 Dr.

ACCOUNT   *Rent Expense*   ACCOUNT NO.   5020

DATE		ITEM	POST. REF.	DEBIT	CREDIT	BALANCE
20— May	1		19	1,540.00		1,540.00 Dr.

PROBLEM 2-9 ___, Continued

ACCOUNT   *Utilities Expense*   ACCOUNT NO.   *5030*

DATE		ITEM	POST. REF.	DEBIT	CREDIT	BALANCE
20— May	30		20	436.60		436.60 Dr.

ACCOUNT   *Advertising Expense*   ACCOUNT NO.   *5040*

DATE		ITEM	POST. REF.	DEBIT	CREDIT	BALANCE
20— May	6		19	275.00		275.00 Dr.

ACCOUNT   *Miscellaneous Expense*   ACCOUNT NO.   *5040*

DATE		ITEM	POST. REF.	DEBIT	CREDIT	BALANCE
20— May	14		19	162.10		162.70 Dr.
	25		20	121.40		283.50 Dr.

PROBLEM 2-9 ___, Continued

HALLMARK ELECTRONIC REPAIR

Unadjusted Trial Balance

May 31, 20—

Cash	9,006.00	
Supplies	99.79	
Land	15,825.00	
Notes Payable		5,600.00
Accounts Payable		1,151.70
Tina Reid, Capital		27,508.70
Tina Reid, Withdrawals		1,350.00
Service Revenue		8,000.40
Wages Expense	3,058.60	
Rent Expense	1,540.00	
Utilities Expense	436.60	
Miscellaneous Expense	283.50	
	30,249.49	43,610.80

PROBLEM 2-9 ___, Continued

Verification Schedule

1. Totals of preliminary trial balance: Debit $ _____

                                                                 Credit $ _____

2. Difference between preliminary trial balance totals: $ _____

3. Errors in trial balance:

_____

_____

_____

_____

_____

_____

4. Errors in account balances:

_____

_____

5. Errors in posting:

_____

_____

_____

_____

_____

_____

_____

_____

6. Journal entry:

JOURNAL   PAGE *19*

	DATE		DESCRIPTION	POST. REF.	DEBIT	CREDIT	
1							1
2							2
3							3
4							4

PROBLEM 2-9 ___, Concluded

7.

HALLMARK ELECTRONIC REPAIR

Unadjusted Trial Balance

May 31, 20—

This page not used.

PROBLEM 2-10 ___

1.

Corrected Unadjusted Trial Balance		
	Debit Balances	Credit Balances
Cash		
Accounts Receivable		
Supplies		
Equipment		
Notes Payable		
Accounts Payable		
_____, Capital		
_____, Withdrawals		
Fees Earned		
Wages Expense		
Rent Expense		
Advertising Expense		
Gas, Electricity, and Water Expense		
Miscellaneous Expense		

2.

This page not used.

PROBLEM 2-11___

a.

Cash

Accounts Receivable

b.

Accounts Receivable

Fees Earned

PROBLEM 2-11___, Concluded

c.

	Supplies

	Cash

d.

	Accounts Payable

	Supplies

PROBLEM 2-12___

	DATE		DESCRIPTION	POST. REF.	DEBIT	CREDIT	
1							1
2							2
3							3
4							4
5							5
6							6
7							7
8							8
9							9
10							10
11							11
12							12
13							13
14							14
15							15
16							16
17							17
18							18
19							19
20							20
21							21
22							22
23							23
24							24
25							25
26							26
27							27
28							28
29							29
30							30
31							31
32							32

JOURNAL   PAGE *18*

This page not used.

CONTINUING PROBLEM

2.

JOURNAL   PAGE *1*

	DATE		DESCRIPTION	POST. REF.	DEBIT	CREDIT	
1							1
2							2
3							3
4							4
5							5
6							6
7							7
8							8
9							9
10							10
11							11
12							12
13							13
14							14
15							15
16							16
17							17
18							18
19							19
20							20
21							21
22							22
23							23
24							24
25							25
26							26
27							27
28							28
29							29
30							30
31							31
32							32
33							33
34							34
35							35
36							36

CONTINUING PROBLEM, Continued

1. and 3.

GENERAL LEDGER

ACCOUNT   *Cash*   ACCOUNT NO.   *1010*

DATE		ITEM	POST. REF.	DEBIT	CREDIT	BALANCE

ACCOUNT   *Accounts Receivable*   ACCOUNT NO.   *1020*

DATE		ITEM	POST. REF.	DEBIT	CREDIT	BALANCE

CONTINUING PROBLEM, Continued

ACCOUNT   *Prepaid Insurance*   ACCOUNT NO.   *1030*

DATE		ITEM	POST. REF.	DEBIT	CREDIT	BALANCE

ACCOUNT   *Supplies*   ACCOUNT NO.   *1040*

DATE		ITEM	POST. REF.	DEBIT	CREDIT	BALANCE

ACCOUNT   *Office Equipment*   ACCOUNT NO.   *1070*

DATE		ITEM	POST. REF.	DEBIT	CREDIT	BALANCE

ACCOUNT   *Accounts Payable*   ACCOUNT NO.   *2010*

DATE		ITEM	POST. REF.	DEBIT	CREDIT	BALANCE

ACCOUNT   *Unearned Revenue*   ACCOUNT NO.   *2020*

DATE		ITEM	POST. REF.	DEBIT	CREDIT	BALANCE

CONTINUING PROBLEM, Continued

ACCOUNT   *Pat Sharpe, Capital*   ACCOUNT NO.   *3010*

DATE		ITEM	POST. REF.	DEBIT	CREDIT	BALANCE

ACCOUNT   *Pat Sharpe, Withdrawals*   ACCOUNT NO.   *3020*

DATE		ITEM	POST. REF.	DEBIT	CREDIT	BALANCE

ACCOUNT   *Fees Earned*   ACCOUNT NO.   *4010*

DATE		ITEM	POST. REF.	DEBIT	CREDIT	BALANCE

CONTINUING PROBLEM, Continued

ACCOUNT   *Music Expense*   ACCOUNT NO.   *5040*

DATE		ITEM	POST. REF.	DEBIT	CREDIT	BALANCE

ACCOUNT   *Advertising Expense*   ACCOUNT NO.   *5050*

DATE		ITEM	POST. REF.	DEBIT	CREDIT	BALANCE

CONTINUING PROBLEM, Concluded

4.

	Unadjusted Trial Balance		

EXERCISE 3-1

1. A two-year premium paid on a fire insurance policy: _____

2. Fees earned but not yet received: _____

3. Fees received but not yet earned: _____

4. Salary owed but not yet paid: _____

5. Subscriptions received in advance by a magazine publisher: _____

6. Supplies on hand: _____

7. Taxes owed but payable in the following period: _____

8. Utilities owed but not yet paid: _____

9. Interest earned and not yet received: _____

EXERCISE 3-2

Account	Answer
Accounts Receivable	_Normally requires adjustment (AR)._
Cash	
Interest Payable	
Interest Receivable	
Johann Atkins, Capital	
Land	
Office Equipment	
Prepaid Rent	
Supplies	
Unearned Fees	
Wages Expense	

EXERCISE 3-3

JOURNAL   PAGE

	DATE		DESCRIPTION	POST. REF.	DEBIT	CREDIT	
1							1
2							2
3							3
4							1
5							2
6							3
7							4
8							4

EXERCISE 3-4

_____

_____

EXERCISE 3-5

JOURNAL   PAGE

	DATE		DESCRIPTION	POST. REF.	DEBIT	CREDIT	
1							1
2							2
3							3
4							4
5							5

EXERCISE 3-6

a. _____

_____

_____

b. _____

_____

_____

EXERCISE 3-7

   a. and b.

JOURNAL   PAGE

	DATE		DESCRIPTION	POST. REF.	DEBIT	CREDIT	
1							1
2							2
3							3
4							4
5							5
6							6

EXERCISE 3-8

a. and b.

	JOURNAL			PAGE	

	DATE		DESCRIPTION	POST. REF.	DEBIT	CREDIT	
1							1
2							2
3							3
4							4
5							5
6							6

EXERCISE 3-9

	JOURNAL			PAGE	

	DATE		DESCRIPTION	POST. REF.	DEBIT	CREDIT	
1							1
2							2
3							3
4							4
5							5
6							6
7							7
8							8
9							9
10							10
11							11
12							12
13							13
14							14
15							15
16							16
17							17
18							18
19							19
20							10
21							21
22							22
23							23
24							24
25							25
26							26

EXERCISE 3-10

a.

		JOURNAL				PAGE

	DATE		DESCRIPTION	POST. REF.	DEBIT	CREDIT	
1							1
2							2
3							3

b.

_____

_____

_____

EXERCISE 3-11

a.

		JOURNAL				PAGE

	DATE		DESCRIPTION	POST. REF.	DEBIT	CREDIT	
1							1
2							2
3							3
4							4
5							5

b.

		JOURNAL				PAGE

	DATE		DESCRIPTION	POST. REF.	DEBIT	CREDIT	
1							1
2							2
3							3
4							4
5							5

EXERCISE 3-12

a.   **JOURNAL**   PAGE

	DATE		DESCRIPTION	POST. REF.	DEBIT	CREDIT	
1							1
2							2
3							3
4							4
5							5

b.   **JOURNAL**   PAGE

	DATE		DESCRIPTION	POST. REF.	DEBIT	CREDIT	
1							1
2							2
3							3
4							4
5							5

EXERCISE 3-13

a. _____

_____

b. _____

_____

EXERCISE 3-14

                                    JOURNAL   PAGE

	DATE		DESCRIPTION	POST. REF.	DEBIT	CREDIT	
1							1
2							2
3							3

EXERCISE 3-15

JOURNAL   PAGE

	DATE	DESCRIPTION	POST. REF.	DEBIT	CREDIT	
1						1
2						2
3						3
4						4
5						5

EXERCISE 3-16

a.

JOURNAL   PAGE

	DATE	DESCRIPTION	POST. REF.	DEBIT	CREDIT	
1						1
2						2
3						3
4						4
5						5

b.

Unearned Revenue:_____

Accounts Receivable:_____

Revenue:_____

EXERCISE 3-17

a. and b.

JOURNAL   PAGE

	DATE	DESCRIPTION	POST. REF.	DEBIT	CREDIT	
1						1
2						2
3						3
4						4
5						5
6						6
7						7

EXERCISE 3-18

a. _____

_____

b. _____

_____

EXERCISE 3-19

a.   **JOURNAL**   PAGE

	DATE		DESCRIPTION	POST. REF.	DEBIT	CREDIT	
1							1
2							2
3							3
4							4
5							5

b.   **JOURNAL**   PAGE

	DATE		DESCRIPTION	POST. REF.	DEBIT	CREDIT	
1							1
2							2
3							3
4							4
5							5

EXERCISE 3-20

a.   JOURNAL   PAGE

	DATE	DESCRIPTION	POST. REF.	DEBIT	CREDIT	
1						1
2						2
3						3
4						4
5						5

b.   JOURNAL   PAGE

	DATE	DESCRIPTION	POST. REF.	DEBIT	CREDIT	
1						1
2						2
3						3
4						4
5						5

EXERCISE 3-21

a., b., c., and d.

JOURNAL   PAGE

	DATE		DESCRIPTION	POST. REF.	DEBIT	CREDIT	
1							1
2							2
3							3
4							4
5							5
6							6
7							7
8							8
9							9
10							10
11							11
12							12
13							13
14							14
15							15
16							16
17							17
18							18

EXERCISE 3-22

_____

_____

_____

EXERCISE 3-23

a.   JOURNAL   PAGE

	DATE		DESCRIPTION	POST. REF.	DEBIT	CREDIT	
1							1
2							2
3							3
4							4
5							5

b.   JOURNAL   PAGE

	DATE		DESCRIPTION	POST. REF.	DEBIT	CREDIT	
1							1
2							2
3							3
4							4
5							5

EXERCISE 3-24

a.   JOURNAL   PAGE

	DATE		DESCRIPTION	POST. REF.	DEBIT	CREDIT	
1							1
2							2
3							3
4							4
5							5

b.   JOURNAL   PAGE

	DATE		DESCRIPTION	POST. REF.	DEBIT	CREDIT	
1							1
2							2
3							3
4							4
5							5

EXERCISE 3-25

a. _____

_____

_____

_____

b. _____

_____

_____

_____

EXERCISE 3-26

a. _____

b. _____

_____

_____

EXERCISE 3-27

a.

JOURNAL

PAGE _____

	DATE		DESCRIPTION	POST. REF.	DEBIT	CREDIT	
1							1
2							2
3							3
4							4
5							5
6							6
7							7

b. _____

_____

EXERCISE 3-28

JOURNAL   PAGE

	DATE		DESCRIPTION	POST. REF.	DEBIT	CREDIT	
1							1
2							2
3							3
4							4
5							5

EXERCISE 3-29

a.

JOURNAL   PAGE

	DATE		DESCRIPTION	POST. REF.	DEBIT	CREDIT	
1							1
2							2
3							3
4							4
5							5

b.

_____

_____

_____

EXERCISE 3-30

a.

JOURNAL PAGE

	DATE		DESCRIPTION	POST. REF.	DEBIT	CREDIT	
1							1
2							2
3							3
4							4
5							5

b.

_____

_____

_____

EXERCISE 3-31

a. _____

b. _____

_____

_____

EXERCISE 3-32

a. _____

b. _____

_____

_____

_____

EXERCISE 3-33

_____

EXERCISE 3-34

_____

EXERCISE 3-35

	Error (a)		Error (b)	
	Overstated	**Understated**	**Overstated**	**Understated**
1. Revenue for the year would be........................	$	$	$	$
2. Expenses for the year would be	$	$	$	$
3. Net income for the year would be...................	$	$	$	$
4. Assets at December 31 would be...................	$	$	$	$
5. Liabilities at December 31 would be...............	$	$	$	$
6. Owner's equity at December 31 would be.......	$	$	$	$

EXERCISE 3-36

_____

EXERCISE 3-37

a.

JOURNAL
PAGE

	DATE	DESCRIPTION	POST. REF.	DEBIT	CREDIT	
1						1
2						2
3						3

b. (1) _____

_____

_____

(2) _____

_____

_____

APPENDIX EXERCISE 3-38

Prepaid Insurance

Insurance Expense

JOURNAL   PAGE

	DATE		DESCRIPTION	POST. REF.	DEBIT	CREDIT	
1							1
2							2
3							3
4							4
5							5
6							6

APPENDIX EXERCISE 3-39

Rent Revenue

Unearned Rent

APPENDIX EXERCISE 3-39, Concluded

JOURNAL   PAGE

	DATE		DESCRIPTION	POST. REF.	DEBIT	CREDIT	
1							1
2							2
3							3

APPENDIX EXERCISE 3-40

a.

Office Supplies

Office Supplies Expense

b.

Office Supplies

Office Supplies Expense

APPENDIX EXERCISE 3-41

a.

	DATE		DESCRIPTION	POST. REF.	DEBIT	CREDIT	
1							1
2							2
3							3

JOURNAL — PAGE

b.

	DATE		DESCRIPTION	POST. REF.	DEBIT	CREDIT	
1							1
2							2
3							3

JOURNAL — PAGE

APPENDIX EXERCISE 3-42

a.

Unearned Advertising Revenue

Advertising Revenue

b.

Unearned Advertising Revenue

Advertising Revenue

APPENDIX EXERCISE 3-43

Unearned Advertising Revenue

Advertising Revenue

JOURNAL

	DATE		DESCRIPTION	POST. REF.	DEBIT	CREDIT	
1							1
2							2
3							3

Unearned Circulation Revenue

Circulation Revenue

JOURNAL

	DATE		DESCRIPTION	POST. REF.	DEBIT	CREDIT	
1							1
2							2
3							3

This page not used.

PROBLEM 3-1 ___

1.

JOURNAL PAGE

	DATE		DESCRIPTION	POST. REF.	DEBIT	CREDIT	
1							1
2							2
3							3
4							4
5							5
6							6
7							7
8							8
9							9
10							10
11							11
12							12
13							13
14							14
15							15
16							16
17							17
18							18
19							19
20							20

2.

This page not used.

PROBLEM 3-2 ___

JOURNAL   PAGE _____

	DATE		DESCRIPTION	POST. REF.	DEBIT	CREDIT	
1							1
2							2
3							3
4							4
5							5
6							6
7							7
8							8
9							9
10							10
11							11
12							12
13							13
14							14
15							15
16							16
17							17
18							18
19							19
20							20
21							21
22							22
23							23
24							24
25							25
26							26
27							27
28							28
29							29
30							30
31							31
32							32
33							33
34							34
35							35
36							36

This Page Not Used.

PROBLEM 3-3 ___

a.

JOURNAL

PAGE _____

	DATE		DESCRIPTION	POST. REF.	DEBIT	CREDIT	
1							1
2							2
3							3
4							4
5							5
6							6
7							7
8							8
9							9
10							10
11							11
12							12
13							13
14							14
15							15
16							16
17							17
18							18
19							19
20							20
21							21
22							22
23							23
24							24
25							25
26							26
27							27
28							28
29							29
30							30
31							31
32							32
33							33
34							34
35							35
36							36

This page not used.

PROBLEM 3-4___

a.

		JOURNAL				PAGE
	DATE	DESCRIPTION	POST. REF.	DEBIT	CREDIT	
1						1
2						2
3						3
4						4
5						5
6						6
7						7
8						8
9						9
10						10
11						11
12						12
13						13
14						14
15						15

PROBLEM 3-4___, Continued

b.

Income Statement

Statement of Owner's Equity

PROBLEM 3-4, ___ Concluded

Balance Sheet

This page not used.

PROBLEM 3-5___

1. _____

_____

_____

_____

2. _____

_____

_____

_____

3. _____

_____

_____

_____

4. _____

_____

_____

_____

5. _____

_____

_____

_____

PROBLEM 3-5 ___, Concluded

Adjusted Trial Balance		

PROBLEM 3-6 ___

1.

		JOURNAL				PAGE

	DATE	DESCRIPTION	POST. REF.	DEBIT	CREDIT	
1						1
2						2
3						3
4						4
5						5
6						6
7						7
8						8
9						9
10						10
11						11
12						12
13						13
14						14
15						15
16						16
17						17
18						18
19						19
20						20
21						21
22						22
23						23
24						24
25						25
26						26
27						27
28						28
29						29
30						30
31						31
32						32
33						33
34						34
35						35
36						36

PROBLEM 3-6 ___, Concluded

2.

Adjusted Trial Balance

PROBLEM 3-7 ___

1.

JOURNAL   PAGE

	DATE		DESCRIPTION	POST. REF.	DEBIT	CREDIT	
1							1
2							2
3							3
4							4
5							5
6							6
7							7
8							8
9							9
10							10
11							11
12							12
13							13
14							14
15							15
16							16
17							17
18							18
19							19
20							20
21							21
22							22
23							23
24							24
25							25
26							26
27							27
28							28
29							29
30							30
31							31
32							32
33							33
34							34
35							35
36							36

PROBLEM 3-7___, Continued

2.

Adjusted Trial Balance		

PROBLEM 3-8 ___

a.

		JOURNAL				PAGE	

	DATE		DESCRIPTION	POST. REF.	DEBIT	CREDIT	
1							1
2							2
3							3
4							4
5							5
6							6
7							7
8							8
9							9
10							10
11							11
12							12
13							13
14							14
15							15
16							16
17							17
18							18
19							19
20							20
21							21
22							22
23							23
24							24
25							25
26							26
27							27
28							28
29							29
30							30
31							31
32							32
33							33
34							34
35							35
36							36

This page not used.

PROBLEM 3-9 ___

1.

<table>
<tr><td colspan="7" align="center">**JOURNAL**   PAGE</td></tr>
<tr>
<th colspan="2">DATE</th>
<th>DESCRIPTION</th>
<th>POST.
REF.</th>
<th>DEBIT</th>
<th>CREDIT</th>
<th></th>
</tr>
<tr><td>1</td><td></td><td></td><td></td><td></td><td></td><td>1</td></tr>
<tr><td>2</td><td></td><td></td><td></td><td></td><td></td><td>2</td></tr>
<tr><td>3</td><td></td><td></td><td></td><td></td><td></td><td>3</td></tr>
<tr><td>4</td><td></td><td></td><td></td><td></td><td></td><td>4</td></tr>
<tr><td>5</td><td></td><td></td><td></td><td></td><td></td><td>5</td></tr>
<tr><td>6</td><td></td><td></td><td></td><td></td><td></td><td>6</td></tr>
<tr><td>7</td><td></td><td></td><td></td><td></td><td></td><td>7</td></tr>
<tr><td>8</td><td></td><td></td><td></td><td></td><td></td><td>8</td></tr>
<tr><td>9</td><td></td><td></td><td></td><td></td><td></td><td>9</td></tr>
<tr><td>10</td><td></td><td></td><td></td><td></td><td></td><td>10</td></tr>
<tr><td>11</td><td></td><td></td><td></td><td></td><td></td><td>11</td></tr>
<tr><td>12</td><td></td><td></td><td></td><td></td><td></td><td>12</td></tr>
<tr><td>13</td><td></td><td></td><td></td><td></td><td></td><td>13</td></tr>
<tr><td>14</td><td></td><td></td><td></td><td></td><td></td><td>14</td></tr>
<tr><td>15</td><td></td><td></td><td></td><td></td><td></td><td>15</td></tr>
<tr><td>16</td><td></td><td></td><td></td><td></td><td></td><td>16</td></tr>
<tr><td>17</td><td></td><td></td><td></td><td></td><td></td><td>17</td></tr>
<tr><td>18</td><td></td><td></td><td></td><td></td><td></td><td>18</td></tr>
<tr><td>19</td><td></td><td></td><td></td><td></td><td></td><td>19</td></tr>
<tr><td>20</td><td></td><td></td><td></td><td></td><td></td><td>20</td></tr>
<tr><td>21</td><td></td><td></td><td></td><td></td><td></td><td>21</td></tr>
<tr><td>22</td><td></td><td></td><td></td><td></td><td></td><td>22</td></tr>
<tr><td>23</td><td></td><td></td><td></td><td></td><td></td><td>23</td></tr>
<tr><td>24</td><td></td><td></td><td></td><td></td><td></td><td>24</td></tr>
<tr><td>25</td><td></td><td></td><td></td><td></td><td></td><td>25</td></tr>
<tr><td>26</td><td></td><td></td><td></td><td></td><td></td><td>26</td></tr>
<tr><td>27</td><td></td><td></td><td></td><td></td><td></td><td>27</td></tr>
<tr><td>28</td><td></td><td></td><td></td><td></td><td></td><td>28</td></tr>
<tr><td>29</td><td></td><td></td><td></td><td></td><td></td><td>29</td></tr>
<tr><td>30</td><td></td><td></td><td></td><td></td><td></td><td>30</td></tr>
<tr><td>31</td><td></td><td></td><td></td><td></td><td></td><td>31</td></tr>
<tr><td>32</td><td></td><td></td><td></td><td></td><td></td><td>32</td></tr>
<tr><td>33</td><td></td><td></td><td></td><td></td><td></td><td>33</td></tr>
<tr><td>34</td><td></td><td></td><td></td><td></td><td></td><td>34</td></tr>
<tr><td>35</td><td></td><td></td><td></td><td></td><td></td><td>35</td></tr>
<tr><td>36</td><td></td><td></td><td></td><td></td><td></td><td>36</td></tr>
</table>

PROBLEM 3-9 ___, Continued

2.

	Adjusted Trial Balance		

PROBLEM 3-9 ___, Continued

Income Statement

Statement of Owner's Equity

PROBLEM 3-9____, Concluded

Balance Sheet

PROBLEM 3-10 ___

1.

JOURNAL   PAGE ____

	DATE		DESCRIPTION	POST. REF.	DEBIT	CREDIT	
1							1
2							2
3							3
4							4
5							5
6							6
7							7
8							8
9							9
10							10
11							11
12							12
13							13
14							14
15							15
16							16

2.

	Net Income	Total Assets	Total Liabilities	Total Owner's Equity
Reported amounts	$ $135,800	$ 75,000	$ 250,000	$ 500,000
Corrections:				
Adjustment (a)	+6,700	+6,700	0	+6,700
Adjustment (b)				
Adjustment (c)				
Adjustment (d)				
Corrected amounts	$	$	$	$

This page not used.

PROBLEM 3-11 ___

1.

JOURNAL   PAGE

	DATE		DESCRIPTION	POST. REF.	DEBIT	CREDIT	
1							1
2							2
3							3
4							4
5							5
6							6
7							7
8							8
9							9
10							10
11							11
12							12
13							13
14							14
15							15
16							16
17							17
18							18
19							19
20							20
21							21
22							22
23							23
24							24
25							25
26							26
27							27
28							28
29							29
30							30
31							31
32							32
33							33
34							34
35							35
36							36

PROBLEM 3-11 ___ , Continued
2.

Adjusted Trial Balance		

PROBLEM 3-11 ___, Continued

3.

JOURNAL   PAGE

	DATE		DESCRIPTION	POST. REF.	DEBIT	CREDIT	
1							1
2							2
3							3
4							4
5							5
6							6
7							7
8							8
9							9
10							10
11							11
12							12
13							13
14							14
15							15
16							16
17							17
18							18
19							19
20							20
21							21
22							22
23							23
24							24
25							25
26							26
27							27
28							28
29							29
30							30
31							31
32							32
33							33
34							34
35							35
36							36

PROBLEM 3-11 ___ , Concluded

4.

Adjusted Trial Balance

APPENDIX PROBLEM 3-12 ___

JOURNAL

	DATE		DESCRIPTION	POST. REF.	DEBIT	CREDIT	
1							1
2							2
3							3
4							4
5							5
6							6
7							7
8							8
9							9
10							10
11							11
12							12
13							13
14							14
15							15
16							16
17							17
18							18
19							19
20							20
21							21
22							22
23							23
24							24

This page not used.

CONTINUING PROBLEM

1.

JOURNAL   PAGE 3

	DATE		DESCRIPTION	POST. REF.	DEBIT	CREDIT	
1							1
2							2
3							3
4							4
5							5
6							6
7							7
8							8
9							9
10							10
11							11
12							12
13							13
14							14
15							15
16							16
17							17
18							18
19							19
20							20
21							21
22							22
23							23
24							24
25							25
26							26
27							27
28							28
29							29
30							30
31							31
32							32
33							33
34							34
35							35
36							36

CONTINUING PROBLEM, Continued

2.

GENERAL LEDGER

ACCOUNT   *Cash*   ACCOUNT NO.   *1010*

DATE		ITEM	POST. REF.	DEBIT	CREDIT	BALANCE

ACCOUNT   *Accounts Receivable*   ACCOUNT NO.   *1020*

DATE		ITEM	POST. REF.	DEBIT	CREDIT	BALANCE

ACCOUNT   *Prepaid Insurance*   ACCOUNT NO.   *1030*

DATE		ITEM	POST. REF.	DEBIT	CREDIT	BALANCE

CONTINUING PROBLEM, Continued

ACCOUNT   *Supplies*   ACCOUNT NO.   *1040*

DATE		ITEM	POST. REF.	DEBIT	CREDIT	BALANCE

ACCOUNT   *Office Equipment*   ACCOUNT NO.   *1070*

DATE		ITEM	POST. REF.	DEBIT	CREDIT	BALANCE

ACCOUNT   *Accumulated Depreciation – Office Equipment*   ACCOUNT NO.   *1080*

DATE		ITEM	POST. REF.	DEBIT	CREDIT	BALANCE

ACCOUNT   *Accounts Payable*   ACCOUNT NO.   *2010*

DATE		ITEM	POST. REF.	DEBIT	CREDIT	BALANCE

ACCOUNT   *Unearned Revenue*   ACCOUNT NO.   *2020*

DATE		ITEM	POST. REF.	DEBIT	CREDIT	BALANCE

CONTINUING PROBLEM, Continued

ACCOUNT   *Wages Payable*   ACCOUNT NO.   *2030*

DATE		ITEM	POST. REF.	DEBIT	CREDIT	BALANCE

ACCOUNT   *Pat Sharpe, Capital*   ACCOUNT NO.   *3010*

DATE		ITEM	POST. REF.	DEBIT	CREDIT	BALANCE

ACCOUNT   *Pat Sharpe, Withdrawals*   ACCOUNT NO.   *3020*

DATE		ITEM	POST. REF.	DEBIT	CREDIT	BALANCE

ACCOUNT   *Income Summary*   ACCOUNT NO.   *3030*

DATE		ITEM	POST. REF.	DEBIT	CREDIT	BALANCE

ACCOUNT   *Fees Earned*   ACCOUNT NO.   *4010*

DATE		ITEM	POST. REF.	DEBIT	CREDIT	BALANCE

CONTINUING PROBLEM, Continued

ACCOUNT   *Music Expense*   ACCOUNT NO.   *5040*

DATE		ITEM	POST. REF.	DEBIT	CREDIT	BALANCE

ACCOUNT   *Advertising Expense*   ACCOUNT NO.   *5050*

DATE		ITEM	POST. REF.	DEBIT	CREDIT	BALANCE

ACCOUNT   *Supplies Expense*   ACCOUNT NO.   *5060*

DATE		ITEM	POST. REF.	DEBIT	CREDIT	BALANCE

ACCOUNT   *Depreciation Expense*   ACCOUNT NO.   *5080*

DATE		ITEM	POST. REF.	DEBIT	CREDIT	BALANCE

CONTINUING PROBLEM, Continued

ACCOUNT   *Insurance Expense*   ACCOUNT NO.   *5090*

DATE		ITEM	POST. REF.	DEBIT	CREDIT	BALANCE

ACCOUNT   *Wages Expense*   ACCOUNT NO.   *5100*

DATE		ITEM	POST. REF.	DEBIT	CREDIT	BALANCE

CONTINUING PROBLEM, Concluded

3.

Adjusted Trial Balance		

Notes

EXERCISE 4-1

a. _____

b. _____

c. _____

d. _____

e. _____

f. _____

g. _____

h. _____

i. _____

j. _____

EXERCISE 4-2

1. Accounts Payable: _____

2. Accounts Receivable: _____

3. Cash: _____

4. Dean Pinkerton, Withdrawals: _____

5. Fees Earned: _____

6. Supplies: _____

7. Unearned Rent: _____

8. Utilities Expense: _____

9. Wages Expense: _____

10. Wages Payable: _____

11. Patents: _____

12. Mortgage Payable: _____

EXERCISE 4-3

1. Accounts Payable: _____

2. Equipment: _____

3. Fees Earned: _____

4. Insurance Expense: _____

5. Prepaid Advertising: _____

6. Prepaid Insurance: _____

7. Rent Revenue: _____

8. Salary Expense: _____

9. Salary Payable: _____

10. Supplies: _____

11. Supplies Expense: _____

12. Unearned Rent: _____

EXERCISE 4-4

	Income Statement		

EXERCISE 4-5

	Income Statement		

EXERCISE 4-6

a.

		Income Statement		

b.

EXERCISE 4-7

Statement of Owner's Equity		

EXERCISE 4-8

	Statement of Owner's Equity		

EXERCISE 4-9

1. Accounts receivable: _____

2. Building: _____

3. Cash: _____

4. Unearned revenue: _____

5. Wages expense: _____

6. Equipment: _____

7. Prepaid rent: _____

8. Supplies: _____

9. Trademarks: _____

10. Investments: _____

EXERCISE 4-10

_____
_____
_____
_____
_____
_____
_____
_____
_____
_____
_____
_____
_____
_____
_____
_____

EXERCISE 4-11

Balance Sheet

EXERCISE 4-12

1. _____

   _____

   _____

   _____

2. _____

   _____

   _____

   _____

3. _____

   _____

   _____

   _____

4. _____

   _____

   _____

   _____

5. _____

   _____

   _____

   _____

6. _____

   _____

   _____

   _____

7. _____

   _____

   _____

   _____

8. _____

   _____

   _____

   _____

   _____

EXERCISE 4-12, Concluded

Balance Sheet

EXERCISE 4-13

a. Accounts Receivable: _____

b. Accumulated Depreciation—Equipment: _____

c. Depreciation Expense—Equipment: _____

d. Equipment: _____

e. Erin Dowley, Capital: _____

f. Erin Dowley, Withdrawals: _____

g. Fees Earned: _____

h. Land: _____

i. Supplies: _____

j. Supplies Expense: _____

k. Wages Expense: _____

l. Wages Payable: _____

EXERCISE 4-14

_____

_____

_____

_____

_____

_____

_____

EXERCISE 4-15

a.

JOURNAL   PAGE

	DATE		DESCRIPTION	POST. REF.	DEBIT	CREDIT	
1							1
2							2
3							3
4							4
5							5
6							6

b. _____

EXERCISE 4-16

a.

JOURNAL   PAGE

	DATE		DESCRIPTION	POST. REF.	DEBIT	CREDIT	
1							1
2							2
3							3
4							4
5							5
6							6
7							7
8							8
9							9
10							10
11							11
12							12

b. _____

EXERCISE 4-17

		JOURNAL			PAGE	

	DATE	DESCRIPTION	POST. REF.	DEBIT	CREDIT	
1						1
2						2
3						3
4						4
5						5
6						6
7						7
8						8
9						9
10						10
11						11
12						12
13						13
14						14

EXERCISE 4-18

JOURNAL   PAGE

	DATE		DESCRIPTION	POST. REF.	DEBIT	CREDIT	
1							1
2							2
3							3
4							4
5							5
6							6
7							7
8							8
9							9
10							10
11							11
12							12
13							13
14							14

EXERCISE 4-19

a. Accounts Payable: _____

b. Accumulated Depreciation: _____

c. Bo Erath, Capital: _____

d. Bo Erath, Withdrawals: _____

e. Cash: _____

f. Depreciation Expense: _____

g. Fees Earned: _____

h. Office Equipment: _____

i. Salaries Expense: _____

j. Salaries Payable: _____

k. Supplies: _____

EXERCISE 4-20

Post-Closing Trial Balance		

APPENDIX 1 EXERCISE 4-21

JOURNAL   PAGE

	DATE		DESCRIPTION	POST. REF.	DEBIT	CREDIT	
1							1
2							2
3							3
4							4

APPENDIX 1 EXERCISE 4-22

a.

JOURNAL

PAGE

	DATE		DESCRIPTION	POST. REF.	DEBIT	CREDIT	
1							1
2							2
3							3
4							4

b.

JOURNAL

PAGE

	DATE		DESCRIPTION	POST. REF.	DEBIT	CREDIT	
1							1
2							2
3							3
4							4

APPENDIX 1 EXERCISE 4-23

1.

JOURNAL

PAGE

	DATE		DESCRIPTION	POST. REF.	DEBIT	CREDIT	
1							1
2							2
3							3
4							4
5							5
6							6
7							75

2.

JOURNAL

PAGE

	DATE		DESCRIPTION	POST. REF.	DEBIT	CREDIT	
1							1
2							2
3							3
4							4
5							5
6							6
7							7

APPENDIX 1 EXERCISE 4-24

1.

JOURNAL   PAGE

	DATE		DESCRIPTION	POST. REF.	DEBIT	CREDIT	
1							1
2							2
3							3
4							4
5							5
6							6
7							7

2.

JOURNAL   PAGE

	DATE		DESCRIPTION	POST. REF.	DEBIT	CREDIT	
1							1
2							2
3							3
4							4
5							5
6							6
7							7

APPENDIX 1 EXERCISE 4-25

a.

1. _____

2. _____

3. _____

4. _____

5. _____

b.

JOURNAL

PAGE

	DATE		DESCRIPTION	POST. REF.	DEBIT	CREDIT	
1							1
2							2
3							3
4							4
5							5
6							6
7							7
8							8
9							9
10							10
11							11
12							12
13							13
14							14
15							15
16							16
17							17
18							18

APPENDIX 1 EXERCISE 4-26

a.

1. _____

2. _____

3. _____

4. _____

5. _____

b.

JOURNAL

PAGE

	DATE	DESCRIPTION	POST. REF.	DEBIT	CREDIT	
1						1
2						2
3						3
4						4
5						5
6						6
7						7
8						8
9						9
10						10
11						11
12						12
13						13
14						14
15						15
16						16
17						17
18						18

APPENDIX 2 EXERCISE 4-27

1. _____   5. _____

2. _____   6. _____

3. _____   7. _____

4. _____   8. _____

APPENDIX 2 EXERCISE 4-28

1. _____
2. _____
3. _____
4. _____
5. _____

6. _____
7. _____
8. _____
9. _____
10. _____

APPENDIX 2 EXERCISE 4-29

_____

_____

_____

_____

_____

APPENDIX 2 EXERCISE 4-30

_____

_____

_____

_____

_____

APPENDIX 2 EXERCISE 4-31

Income Statement

Statement of Owner's Equity

APPENDIX 2 EXERCISE 4-31, Concluded

Balance Sheet

APPENDIX 2 EXERCISE 4-32

	Income Statement		

	Statement of Owner's Equity		

APPENDIX 2 EXERCISE 4-32, Concluded

Balance Sheet

APPENDIX 2 EXERCISE 4-33

1. _____

2. _____

3. _____

4. _____

5. _____

6. _____

7. _____

8. _____

9. _____

10. _____

APPENDIX 2 EXERCISE 4-34

Zeidman's Security Services Co.
End-of-Period Spreadsheet (Work Sheet)
For the Year Ended December 31, 2015
(in $000.5)

	A	B	C	D	E	F	G	H	I	J	K
			Unadjusted Trial Balance		Adjustments		Adjusted Trial Balance				
	Account Title	Dr.	Cr.	Dr.	Cr.	Dr.	Cr.				
7	Cash	12									
8	Accounts Receivable	80									
9	Supplies	8									
10	Prepaid Insurance	12									
11	Equipment	40									
12	Accum. Depr.—Equipment		4								
13	Land	100									
14	Accounts Payable		36								
15	Wages Payable		0								
16	Alex Zeidman, Capital		170								
17	Alex Zeidman, Withdrawals	9									
18	Fees Earned		90								
19	Wages Expense	20									
20	Rent Expense	12									
21	Insurance Expense	0									
22	Utilities Expense	6									
23	Depreciation Expense	0									
24	Supplies Expense	0									
25	Miscellaneous Expense	2									
26	Totals	154	154								
27											
28											
29											

APPENDIX 2 EXERCISE 4-35

Zeidman's Security Services Co.
End-of-Period Spreadsheet (Work Sheet)
For the Year Ended December 31, 2015
(in $000.5)

Account Title	Adjusted Trial Balance		Income Statement		Balance Sheet	
	Dr.	Cr.	Dr.	Cr.	Dr.	Cr.
Cash	12					
Accounts Receivable	89					
Supplies	3					
Prepaid Insurance	4					
Equipment	40					
Accum. Depr.—Equipment		8				
Land	100					
Accounts Payable		36				
Wages Payable		1				
Alex Zeidman, Capital		170				
Alex Zeidman, Withdrawals	8					
Fees Earned		99				
Wages Expense	21					
Rent Expense	12					
Insurance Expense	8					
Utilities Expense	6					
Depreciation Expense	5					
Supplies Expense	4					
Miscellaneous Expense	2					
Totals	314	314				
Net income (loss)						

APPENDIX 2 EXERCISE 4-36

Income Statement

Statement of Owner's Equity

APPENDIX 2 EXERCISE 4-36, Concluded

Balance Sheet

APPENDIX 2 EXERCISE 4-37

JOURNAL

	DATE		DESCRIPTION	POST. REF.	DEBIT	CREDIT	
1							1
2							2
3							3
4							4
5							5
6							6
7							7
8							8
9							9
10							10
11							11
12							12
13							13
14							14
15							15
16							16
17							17
18							18
19							19
20							20

APPENDIX 2 EXERCISE 4-38

JOURNAL

	DATE		DESCRIPTION	POST. REF.	DEBIT	CREDIT	
1							1
2							2
3							3
4							4
5							5
6							6
7							7
8							8
9							9
10							10
11							11
12							12
13							13
14							14
15							15
16							16
17							17
18							18
19							19
20							20

PROBLEM 4-1 ___

1.

<table>
<tr><td colspan="3" align="center">*Income Statement*</td></tr>
<tr><td></td><td></td><td></td></tr>
<tr><td></td><td></td><td></td></tr>
<tr><td></td><td></td><td></td></tr>
<tr><td></td><td></td><td></td></tr>
<tr><td></td><td></td><td></td></tr>
<tr><td></td><td></td><td></td></tr>
<tr><td></td><td></td><td></td></tr>
<tr><td></td><td></td><td></td></tr>
<tr><td></td><td></td><td></td></tr>
<tr><td></td><td></td><td></td></tr>
<tr><td></td><td></td><td></td></tr>
</table>

2.

<table>
<tr><td colspan="3" align="center">*Statement of Owner's Equity*</td></tr>
<tr><td></td><td></td><td></td></tr>
<tr><td></td><td></td><td></td></tr>
<tr><td></td><td></td><td></td></tr>
<tr><td></td><td></td><td></td></tr>
<tr><td></td><td></td><td></td></tr>
<tr><td></td><td></td><td></td></tr>
<tr><td></td><td></td><td></td></tr>
</table>

PROBLEM 4-1 _____, Continued

3.

Balance Sheet

PROBLEM 4-1 ___, Continued

4.

JOURNAL

	DATE		DESCRIPTION	POST. REF.	DEBIT	CREDIT	
1							1
2							2
3							3
4							4
5							5
6							6
7							7
8							8
9							9
10							10
11							11
12							12
13							13
14							14

PROBLEM 4-1 ___ , Concluded

5.

Post-Closing Trial Balance		

PROBLEM 4-2 ___

1.

Income Statement		

2.

Statement of Owner's Equity		

PROBLEM 4-2 ____, Continued

3.

Balance Sheet

PROBLEM 4-2 ____, Continued

4.

JOURNAL   PAGE

	DATE		DESCRIPTION	POST. REF.	DEBIT	CREDIT	
1							1
2							2
3							3
4							4
5							5
6							6
7							7
8							8
9							9
10							10
11							11
12							12
13							13
14							14
15							15
16							16

PROBLEM 4-2 ___ , Concluded

5.

Post-Closing Trial Balance		

PROBLEM 4-3 ___

1.

Income Statement

Statement of Owner's Equity

PROBLEM 4-3 _____, Continued

Balance Sheet

PROBLEM 4-3 ___, Concluded

2.

JOURNAL   PAGE

	DATE		DESCRIPTION	POST. REF.	DEBIT	CREDIT	
1							1
2							2
3							3
4							4
5							5
6							6
7							7
8							8
9							9
10							10
11							11
12							12
13							13
14							14
15							15
16							16
17							17
18							18
19							19
20							20
21							21

3.

This page not used.

PROBLEM 4-4 ___

1.

Cash

Laundry Supplies

Prepaid Insurance

Laundry Equipment

Accumulated Depreciation – Laundry Equipment

Accounts Payable

Wages Payable

_____, Capital

PROBLEM 4-4 ___, Continued

_____, *Withdrawals*

Income Summary

Laundry Revenue

Wages Expense

Rent Expense

Utilities Expense

Depreciation Expense

Laundry Supplies Expense

Insurance Expense

Miscellaneous Expense

PROBLEM 4-4 ___, Continued

2.

JOURNAL   PAGE

	DATE		DESCRIPTION	POST. REF.	DEBIT	CREDIT	
1			*Adjusting Entries*				1
2							2
3							3
4							4
5							5
6							6
7							7
8							8
9							9
10							10
11							11
12							12
13							13
14							14
15							15
16							16

PROBLEM 4-4 ___, Continued

3.

Adjusted Trial Balance		

PROBLEM 4-4 ___, Continued

4.

	Income Statement		

	Statement of Owner's Equity		

PROBLEM 4-4 _____, Continued

Balance Sheet

PROBLEM 4-4 ___, Concluded

5.

JOURNAL   PAGE

	DATE	DESCRIPTION	POST. REF.	DEBIT	CREDIT	
1		*Closing Entries*				1
2						2
3						3
4						4
5						5
6						6
7						7
8						8
9						9
10						10
11						11
12						12
13						13
14						14
15						15
16						16
17						17
18						18
19						19

6.

Post-Closing Trial Balance

This page not used.

PROBLEM 4-5A

1.   **Optional**

Account Title	Unadjusted Trial Balance Dr.	Cr.
Cash	26,870	
Accounts Receivable	10,900	
Supplies	3,050	
Prepaid Insurance	4,800	
Building	312,000	
Accum. Depr.—Building		
Equipment	150,000	
Accum. Depr..—Equipment		
Land	50,000	
Accounts Payable		3,350
Wages Payable		
Unearned Rent		2,700
Young Lee, Capital		529,100
Young Lee, Withdrawals	2,000	
Service Revenue		35,000
Rent Revenue		
Wages Expense	5,000	
Supplies Expense		
Rent Expense	2,500	
Depreciation Expense		
Utilities Expense	1,650	
Insurance Expense		
Misc. Expense	1,380	
	570,150	570,150

PROBLEM 4-5A, Continued

1.

JOURNAL

	DATE		DESCRIPTION	POST. REF.	DEBIT	CREDIT	
1			*Adjusting Entries*				1
2							2
3							3
4							4
5							5
6							6
7							7
8							8
9							9
10							10
11							11
12							12
13							13
14							14
15							15
16							16
17							17
18							18
19							19
20							20
21							21
22							22
23							23
24							24
25							25
26							26
27							27
28							28
29							29
30							30
31							31
32							32
33							33
34							34
35							35
36							36

PROBLEM 4-5A, Continued

2.

Adjusted Trial Balance		

PROBLEM 4-5A, Continued

3.

	Income Statement		

	Statement of Owner's Equity		

PROBLEM 4-5A, Continued

Balance Sheet

PROBLEM 4-5A, Continued

4.

		JOURNAL			PAGE 27

	DATE		DESCRIPTION	POST. REF.	DEBIT	CREDIT	
1			*Closing Entries*				1
2							2
3							3
4							4
5							5
6							6
7							7
8							8
9							9
10							10
11							11
12							12
13							13
14							14
15							15
16							16
17							17
18							18
19							19
20							20
21							21
22							22
23							23
24							24
25							25
26							26
27							27
28							28
29							29
30							30
31							31
32							32
33							33
34							34
35							35
36							36

PROBLEM 4-5A, Continued

5.

	Post-Closing Trial Balance		

PROBLEM 4-5A, Continued

1. and 4.

ACCOUNT   *Cash*   ACCOUNT NO.   *1010*

DATE		ITEM	POST. REF.	DEBIT	CREDIT	BALANCE
2012 Dec.	1	Balance	√			6,000.00 Dr.
	3		23		2,500.00	3,500.00 Dr.
	4		23	5,000.00		8,500.00 Dr.
	5		23		400.00	8,100.00 Dr.
	7		23	3,200.00		11,300.00 Dr.
	8		23	5,900.00		17,200.00 Dr.
	8		23		4,500.00	12,700.00 Dr.
	8		23	9,400.00		22,100.00 Dr.
	10		24		500.00	21,600.00 Dr.
	12		24		2,400.00	19,200.00 Dr.
	15		24	7,800.00		27,000.00 Dr.
	16		24		1,000.00	26,000.00 Dr.
	19		24		2,100.00	23,900.00 Dr.
	22		24		1,200.00	22,700.00 Dr.
	22		24	8,100.00		30,800.00 Dr.
	24		25		800.00	30,000.00 Dr.
	26		25		2,600.00	27,400.00 Dr.
	30		25		350.00	27,050.00 Dr.
	30		25		600.00	26,450.00 Dr.
	31		25		1,000.00	25,450.00 Dr.
	31		25	2,200.00		27,650.00 Dr.
	31		25		780.00	26,870.00 Dr.

PROBLEM 4-5A, Continued

ACCOUNT   *Accounts Receivable*   ACCOUNT NO.   *1020*

DATE		ITEM	POST. REF.	DEBIT	CREDIT	BALANCE
2012 Dec.	1	Balance	√			12,500.00 Dr.
	7		23		3,200.00	9,300.00 Dr.
	8		23		5,900.00	3,400.00 Dr.
	22		24	7,500.00		10,900.00 Dr.

ACCOUNT   *Supplies*   ACCOUNT NO.   *1030*

DATE		ITEM	POST. REF.	DEBIT	CREDIT	BALANCE
2012 Dec.	1	Balance	√			1,750.00 Dr.
	10		24	500.00		2,2500.0 Dr.
	27		25	800.00		3,050.00 Dr.

ACCOUNT   *Prepaid Insurance*   ACCOUNT NO.   *1040*

DATE		ITEM	POST. REF.	DEBIT	CREDIT	BALANCE
2012 Dec	1	Balance	√			3,600.00 Dr.
	22		24	1,200.00		4,800.00 Dr.

PROBLEM 4-5A, Continued

ACCOUNT   *Building*   ACCOUNT NO.   *1050*

DATE		ITEM	POST. REF.	DEBIT	CREDIT	BALANCE
2012 Dec.	1	Balance	√			312, 000.00 Dr.

ACCOUNT   *Accumulated Amortization—Building*   ACCOUNT NO.   *1060*

DATE		ITEM	POST. REF.	DEBIT	CREDIT	BALANCE
2012 Dec.	1	Balance	√			0 Cr.

ACCOUNT   *Equipment*   ACCOUNT NO.   *1070*

DATE		ITEM	POST. REF.	DEBIT	CREDIT	BALANCE
2012 Dec.	1	Balance	√			147, 250.00 Dr.
	3		23	2,750.00		150,000.00 Dr.

ACCOUNT   *Accumulated Amortization—Equipment*   ACCOUNT NO.   *1080*

DATE		ITEM	POST. REF.	DEBIT	CREDIT	BALANCE
2012 Dec.	1	Balance	√			0 Cr.

PROBLEM 4-5A, Continued

ACCOUNT   *Land*   ACCOUNT NO.   *1090*

DATE		ITEM	POST. REF.	DEBIT	CREDIT	BALANCE
2012 Dec.	1	*Balance*	√			50,000.00 Dr.

ACCOUNT   *Accounts Payable*   ACCOUNT NO.   *2010*

DATE		ITEM	POST. REF.	DEBIT	CREDIT	BALANCE
2012 Dec.	1	*Balance*	√			6,300.00 Cr.
	3		23		2,750.00	9,050.00 Cr.
	8		23	4,500.00		4,550.00 Cr.
	19		24	2,100.00		2,450.00 Cr.
	31		25		900.00	3,350.00 Cr.

ACCOUNT   *Wages Payable*   ACCOUNT NO.   *2020*

DATE		ITEM	POST. REF.	DEBIT	CREDIT	BALANCE

ACCOUNT   *Unearned Rent*   ACCOUNT NO.   *2030*

DATE		ITEM	POST. REF.	DEBIT	CREDIT	BALANCE
2012 Dec.	1	*Balance*	√			2,700.00 Cr.

PROBLEM 4-5A, Continued

ACCOUNT　*Young Lee, Capital*　　　　ACCOUNT NO.　3010

DATE		ITEM	POST. REF.	DEBIT	CREDIT	BALANCE
2012 Dec.	1	Balance	√			524,100.00 Cr.
	4	23	23		5,000.00	529,100.00 Cr.

ACCOUNT　*Young Lee, Withdrawals*　　　　ACCOUNT NO.　3020

DATE		ITEM	POST. REF.	DEBIT	CREDIT	BALANCE
2012 Dec.	16		24	1,000.00		1,000.00 Dr.
	31		25	1,000.00		2,000.00 Dr.

ACCOUNT　*Income Summary*　　　　ACCOUNT NO.　3030

DATE		ITEM	POST. REF.	DEBIT	CREDIT	BALANCE

PROBLEM 4-5A, Continued

ACCOUNT   *Service Revenue*   ACCOUNT NO.   *4010*

DATE		ITEM	POST. REF.	DEBIT	CREDIT	BALANCE
2012 Dec.	8		23		9,400.00	9,400.00 Cr.
	15		24		7,800.00	17,200.00 Cr.
	22		24		8,100.00	25,300.00 Cr.
	22		24		7,500.00	32,800.00 Cr.
	31		25		2,200.00	35,000.00 Cr.

ACCOUNT   *Rent Revenue*   ACCOUNT NO.   *4020*

DATE	ITEM	POST. REF.	DEBIT	CREDIT	BALANCE

ACCOUNT   *Wages Expense*   ACCOUNT NO.   *5010*

DATE		ITEM	POST. REF.	DEBIT	CREDIT	BALANCE
2012 Dec.	12		24	2,400.00		2,400.00 Dr.
	26		25	2,600.00		5,000.00 Dr.

PROBLEM 4-5A, Continued

ACCOUNT   *Supplies Expense*   ACCOUNT NO.   *5020*

DATE		ITEM	POST. REF.	DEBIT	CREDIT	BALANCE

ACCOUNT   *Rent Expense*   ACCOUNT NO.   *5030*

DATE		ITEM	POST. REF.	DEBIT	CREDIT	BALANCE
2012 Dec.	3		23	2,500.00		2,500.00 Dr.

ACCOUNT   *Depreciation Expense*   ACCOUNT NO.   *5040*

DATE		ITEM	POST. REF.	DEBIT	CREDIT	BALANCE

PROBLEM 4-5A, Concluded

ACCOUNT   *Utilities Expense*   ACCOUNT NO.   *5050*

DATE		ITEM	POST. REF.	DEBIT	CREDIT	BALANCE
2012 Dec.	5		24	400.00		400.00 Dr.
	30		25	350.00		750.00 Dr.
	31		25	900.00		1,650.00 Dr.

ACCOUNT   *Insurance Expense*   ACCOUNT NO.   *5070*

DATE		ITEM	POST. REF.	DEBIT	CREDIT	BALANCE

ACCOUNT   *Miscellaneous Expense*   ACCOUNT NO.   *5090*

DATE		ITEM	POST. REF.	DEBIT	CREDIT	BALANCE
2012 Dec.	30		25	600.00		600.00 Dr..
	31		25	780.00		1,380.00 Dr

This page not used.

PROBLEM 4-6 ___

2.

| | JOURNAL | | | | PAGE 26 |

	DATE		DESCRIPTION	POST. REF.	DEBIT	CREDIT	
1			*Adjusting Entries*				1
2							2
3							3
4							4
5							5
6							6
7							7
8							8
9							9
10							10
11							11
12							12
13							13
14							14
15							15
16							16
17							17
18							18
19							19
20							20

PROBLEM 4-6 ___ , Continued

3.

Adjusted Trial Balance		

PROBLEM 4-6 ___, Continued

4.

Income Statement			

Statement of Owner's Equity			

PROBLEM 4-6 ____, Continued

Balance Sheet

PROBLEM 4-6 ___, Continued

1., 2., and 5.

ACCOUNT   *Cash*   ACCOUNT NO.   *1010*

DATE		ITEM	POST. REF.	DEBIT	CREDIT	BALANCE

ACCOUNT   *Supplies*   ACCOUNT NO.   *1030*

DATE		ITEM	POST. REF.	DEBIT	CREDIT	BALANCE

ACCOUNT   *Prepaid Insurance*   ACCOUNT NO.   *1040*

DATE		ITEM	POST. REF.	DEBIT	CREDIT	BALANCE

ACCOUNT   *Equipment*   ACCOUNT NO.   *1060*

DATE		ITEM	POST. REF.	DEBIT	CREDIT	BALANCE

ACCOUNT   *Accumulated Depreciation—Equipment*   ACCOUNT NO.   *1070*

DATE		ITEM	POST. REF.	DEBIT	CREDIT	BALANCE

PROBLEM 4-6 ___ , Continued

ACCOUNT   *Trucks*   ACCOUNT NO.   *1080*

DATE	ITEM	POST. REF.	DEBIT	CREDIT	BALANCE

ACCOUNT   *Accumulated Depreciation—Trucks*   ACCOUNT NO.   *1090*

DATE	ITEM	POST. REF.	DEBIT	CREDIT	BALANCE

ACCOUNT   *Accounts Payable*   ACCOUNT NO.   *2010*

DATE	ITEM	POST. REF.	DEBIT	CREDIT	BALANCE

ACCOUNT   *Wages Payable*   ACCOUNT NO.   *2020*

DATE	ITEM	POST. REF.	DEBIT	CREDIT	BALANCE

ACCOUNT   _____ , *Capital*   ACCOUNT NO.   *3010*

DATE	ITEM	POST. REF.	DEBIT	CREDIT	BALANCE

ACCOUNT   _____ , *Withdrawals*   ACCOUNT NO.   *3020*

DATE	ITEM	POST. REF.	DEBIT	CREDIT	BALANCE

PROBLEM 4-6 ___, Continued

ACCOUNT   *Income Summary*   ACCOUNT NO.   *3030*

DATE		ITEM	POST. REF.	DEBIT	CREDIT	BALANCE

ACCOUNT   *Service Revenue*   ACCOUNT NO.   *4010*

DATE		ITEM	POST. REF.	DEBIT	CREDIT	BALANCE

ACCOUNT   *Wages Expense*   ACCOUNT NO.   *5010*

DATE		ITEM	POST. REF.	DEBIT	CREDIT	BALANCE

ACCOUNT   *Supplies Expense*   ACCOUNT NO.   *5020*

DATE		ITEM	POST. REF.	DEBIT	CREDIT	BALANCE

ACCOUNT   *Rent Expense*   ACCOUNT NO.   *5030*

DATE		ITEM	POST. REF.	DEBIT	CREDIT	BALANCE

PROBLEM 4-6 ___, Continued

ACCOUNT   *Depreciation Expense*   ACCOUNT NO.   *5040*

DATE		ITEM	POST. REF.	DEBIT	CREDIT	BALANCE

ACCOUNT   *Truck Expense*   ACCOUNT NO.   *5050*

DATE		ITEM	POST. REF.	DEBIT	CREDIT	BALANCE

ACCOUNT   *Insurance Expense*   ACCOUNT NO.   *5070*

DATE		ITEM	POST. REF.	DEBIT	CREDIT	BALANCE

ACCOUNT   *Miscellaneous Expense*   ACCOUNT NO.   *5090*

DATE		ITEM	POST. REF.	DEBIT	CREDIT	BALANCE

PROBLEM 4-6 ___ , Concluded

5.

JOURNAL   PAGE *27*

	DATE		DESCRIPTION	POST. REF.	DEBIT	CREDIT	
1			*Closing Entries*				1
2							2
3							3
4							4
5							5
6							6
7							7
8							8
9							9
10							10
11							11
12							12
13							13
14							14
15							15
16							16
17							17
18							18
19							19
20							20

6.

Post-Closing Trial Balance

This page not used.

PROBLEM 4-7 ___

1. and 2.   **JOURNAL**   PAGE   *1*

	DATE		DESCRIPTION	POST. REF.	DEBIT	CREDIT	
1							1
2							2
3							3
4							4
5							5
6							6
7							7
8							8
9							9
10							10
11							11
12							12
13							13
14							14
15							15
16							16
17							17
18							18
19							19
20							20
21							21
22							22
23							23
24							24
25							25
26							26
27							27
28							28
29							29
30							30
31							31
32							32
33							33
34							34
35							35
36							36

PROBLEM 4-7 ___ , Continued

2., 5., and 8.

ACCOUNT   *Cash*   ACCOUNT NO.   *1010*

DATE		ITEM	POST. REF.	DEBIT	CREDIT	BALANCE

ACCOUNT   *Accounts Receivable*   ACCOUNT NO.   *1020*

DATE		ITEM	POST. REF.	DEBIT	CREDIT	BALANCE

PROBLEM 4-7 ___, Continued

ACCOUNT   *Supplies*   ACCOUNT NO.   *1040*

DATE		ITEM	POST. REF.	DEBIT	CREDIT	BALANCE

ACCOUNT   *Prepaid Rent*   ACCOUNT NO.   *1050*

DATE		ITEM	POST. REF.	DEBIT	CREDIT	BALANCE

ACCOUNT   *Prepaid Insurance*   ACCOUNT NO.   *1060*

DATE		ITEM	POST. REF.	DEBIT	CREDIT	BALANCE

ACCOUNT   *Office Equipment*   ACCOUNT NO.   *1080*

DATE		ITEM	POST. REF.	DEBIT	CREDIT	BALANCE

ACCOUNT   *Accumulated Depreciation*   ACCOUNT NO.   *1090*

DATE		ITEM	POST. REF.	DEBIT	CREDIT	BALANCE

PROBLEM 4-7 ___, Continued

ACCOUNT   *Accounts Payable*   ACCOUNT NO.   *2010*

DATE		ITEM	POST. REF.	DEBIT	CREDIT	BALANCE	

ACCOUNT   *Unearned Fees*   ACCOUNT NO.   *2030*

DATE		ITEM	POST. REF.	DEBIT	CREDIT	BALANCE	

ACCOUNT   _____, *Capital*   ACCOUNT NO.   *3010*

DATE		ITEM	POST. REF.	DEBIT	CREDIT	BALANCE	

ACCOUNT   _____, *Withdrawals*   ACCOUNT NO.   *3020*

DATE		ITEM	POST. REF.	DEBIT	CREDIT	BALANCE	

PROBLEM 4-7 ___, Continued

ACCOUNT   *Income Summary*   ACCOUNT NO.   *3030*

DATE		ITEM	POST. REF.	DEBIT	CREDIT	BALANCE	

ACCOUNT   *Fees Earned*   ACCOUNT NO.   *4010*

DATE		ITEM	POST. REF.	DEBIT	CREDIT	BALANCE	

ACCOUNT   *Rent Expense*   ACCOUNT NO.   *5020*

DATE		ITEM	POST. REF.	DEBIT	CREDIT	BALANCE	

PROBLEM 4-7 ___, Continued

ACCOUNT   *Supplies Expense*   ACCOUNT NO.   *5030*

DATE		ITEM	POST. REF.	DEBIT	CREDIT	BALANCE

ACCOUNT   *Depreciation Expense*   ACCOUNT NO.   *5040*

DATE		ITEM	POST. REF.	DEBIT	CREDIT	BALANCE

ACCOUNT   *Insurance Expense*   ACCOUNT NO.   *5050*

DATE		ITEM	POST. REF.	DEBIT	CREDIT	BALANCE

ACCOUNT   *Miscellaneous Expense*   ACCOUNT NO.   *5090*

DATE		ITEM	POST. REF.	DEBIT	CREDIT	BALANCE

PROBLEM 4-7 ___ , Continued

3.

	Unadjusted Trial Balance		

PROBLEM 4-7 ___ , Continued

5.   **JOURNAL**   PAGE 3

	DATE		DESCRIPTION	POST. REF.	DEBIT	CREDIT	
1			*Adjusting Entries*				1
2							2
3							3
4							4
5							5
6							6
7							7
8							8
9							9
10							10
11							11
12							12
13							13
14							14
15							15
16							16
17							17
18							18
19							19
20							20

PROBLEM 4-7 ___ , Continued

6.

Adjusted Trial Balance		

PROBLEM 4-7 ___, Continued

7.

Income Statement

Statement of Owner's Equity

PROBLEM 4-7 _____, Continued

Balance Sheet

PROBLEM 4-7 ___, Concluded

8.

		JOURNAL			PAGE 4

	DATE		DESCRIPTION	POST. REF.	DEBIT	CREDIT	
1			*Closing Entries*				1
2							2
3							3
4							4
5							5
6							6
7							7
8							8
9							9
10							10
11							11
12							12
13							13
14							14
15							15
16							16
17							17
18							18

9.

Post-Closing Trial Balance

PROBLEM 4-8 ___

1. and 2.   **JOURNAL**   PAGE *1*

	DATE		DESCRIPTION	POST. REF.	DEBIT	CREDIT	
1							1
2							2
3							3
4							4
5							5
6							6
7							7
8							8
9							9
10							10
11							11
12							12
13							13
14							14
15							15
16							16
17							17
18							18
19							19
20							20
21							21
22							22
23							23
24							24
25							25
26							26
27							27
28							28
29							29
30							30
31							31
32							32
33							33
34							34
35							35
36							36

PROBLEM 4-8 ___ , Continued

2., 5., and 8.

ACCOUNT   *Cash*   ACCOUNT NO.   *1010*

DATE		ITEM	POST. REF.	DEBIT	CREDIT	BALANCE

ACCOUNT   *Accounts Receivable*   ACCOUNT NO.   *1020*

DATE		ITEM	POST. REF.	DEBIT	CREDIT	BALANCE

PROBLEM 4-8 ___, Continued

ACCOUNT   *Supplies*   ACCOUNT NO.   *1040*

DATE		ITEM	POST. REF.	DEBIT	CREDIT	BALANCE	

ACCOUNT   *Office Equipment*   ACCOUNT NO.   *1080*

DATE		ITEM	POST. REF.	DEBIT	CREDIT	BALANCE	

ACCOUNT   *Accumulated Depreciation*   ACCOUNT NO.   *1090*

DATE		ITEM	POST. REF.	DEBIT	CREDIT	BALANCE	

ACCOUNT   *Accounts Payable*   ACCOUNT NO.   *2010*

DATE		ITEM	POST. REF.	DEBIT	CREDIT	BALANCE	

ACCOUNT   *Salaries Payable*   ACCOUNT NO.   *2020*

DATE		ITEM	POST. REF.	DEBIT	CREDIT	BALANCE	

PROBLEM 4-8 ___ , Continued

ACCOUNT   *Unearned Fees*   ACCOUNT NO.   *2030*

DATE		ITEM	POST. REF.	DEBIT	CREDIT	BALANCE

ACCOUNT   _____ , *Capital*   ACCOUNT NO.   *3010*

DATE		ITEM	POST. REF.	DEBIT	CREDIT	BALANCE

ACCOUNT   _____ , *Withdrawals*   ACCOUNT NO.   *3020*

DATE		ITEM	POST. REF.	DEBIT	CREDIT	BALANCE

PROBLEM 4-8 ___, Continued

ACCOUNT *Income Summary* ACCOUNT NO. *3030*

DATE		ITEM	POST. REF.	DEBIT	CREDIT	BALANCE	

ACCOUNT *Fees Earned* ACCOUNT NO. *4010*

DATE		ITEM	POST. REF.	DEBIT	CREDIT	BALANCE	

ACCOUNT *Salary Expense* ACCOUNT NO. *5010*

DATE		ITEM	POST. REF.	DEBIT	CREDIT	BALANCE	

PROBLEM 4-8 ___, Continued

ACCOUNT   *Supplies Expense*   ACCOUNT NO.   *5030*

DATE		ITEM	POST. REF.	DEBIT	CREDIT	BALANCE	

ACCOUNT   *Depreciation Expense*   ACCOUNT NO.   *5040*

DATE		ITEM	POST. REF.	DEBIT	CREDIT	BALANCE	

PROBLEM 4-8 ___, Continued

3.

	Unadjusted Trial Balance		

PROBLEM 4-8 ___ , Continued

5.   **JOURNAL**   PAGE 3

	DATE		DESCRIPTION	POST. REF.	DEBIT	CREDIT	
1			*Adjusting Entries*				1
2							2
3							3
4							4
5							5
6							6
7							7
8							8
9							9
10							10
11							11
12							12
13							13
14							14
15							15
16							16
17							17
18							18
19							19
20							20

PROBLEM 4-8 ___, Continued

6.

Adjusted Trial Balance		

PROBLEM 4-8 ___ , Continued

7.

Income Statement		

Statement of Owner's Equity		

PROBLEM 4-8 ____, Continued

Balance Sheet

PROBLEM 4-8 ___, Concluded

8.   **JOURNAL**   PAGE *4*

	DATE		DESCRIPTION	POST. REF.	DEBIT	CREDIT	
1			*Closing Entries*				1
2							2
3							3
4							4
5							5
6							6
7							7
8							8
9							9
10							10
11							11
12							12
13							13
14							14
15							15
16							16
17							17
18							18

9.

Post-Closing Trial Balance

APPENDIX 1 PROBLEM 4–9 ____

JOURNAL

	DATE		DESCRIPTION	POST. REF.	DEBIT	CREDIT	
1							1
2							2
3							3
4							4
5							5
6							6
7							7
8							8
9							9
10							10
11							11
12							12
13							13

This page not used.

APPENDIX 1 PROBLEM 4–10 ____

JOURNAL   PAGE

	DATE		DESCRIPTION	POST. REF.	DEBIT	CREDIT	
1							1
2							2
3							3
4							4
5							5
6							6
7							7
8							8
9							9
10							10
11							11
12							12
13							13
14							14
15							15
16							16
17							17
18							18
19							19
20							20
21							21
22							22
23							23
24							24
25							25
26							26
27							27
28							28
29							29
30							30

This page not used.

APPENDIX 2 PROBLEM 4–11 ____

1.

Income Statement		

2.

Statement of Owner's Equity		

APPENDIX 2 PROBLEM 4–11 ____, Continued

3.

Balance Sheet

APPENDIX 2 PROBLEM 4-11 ___ , Continued

4.

JOURNAL   PAGE

	DATE		DESCRIPTION	POST. REF.	DEBIT	CREDIT	
1							1
2							2
3							3
4							4
5							5
6							6
7							7
8							8
9							9
10							10
11							11
12							12
13							13
14							14
15							15
16							16

APPENDIX 2 PROBLEM 4-11 ___ , Concluded

5.

Post-Closing Trial Balance		

APPENDIX 2 PROBLEM 4-12

1.

Income Statement		

Statement of Owner's Equity		

APPENDIX 2 PROBLEM 4–12 ____, Continued

Balance Sheet

APPENDIX 2 PROBLEM 4-12 ___ , Continued

2.

JOURNAL

	DATE		DESCRIPTION	POST. REF.	DEBIT	CREDIT	
1							1
2							2
3							3
4							4
5							5
6							6
7							7
8							8
9							9
10							10
11							11
12							12
13							13
14							14
15							15
16							16

APPENDIX 2 PROBLEM 4-12 ___ , Concluded

3.

_____

_____

_____

_____

APPENDIX 2 PROBLEM 4-13 ___

1.

Cash

Laundry Supplies

Prepaid Insurance

Laundry Equipment

APPENDIX 2 PROBLEM 4-13 ___, Continued

Accumulated Depreciation—Laundry Equipment

Accounts Payable

Wages Payable

_____, *Capital*

_____, *Withdrawals*

Income Summary

Laundry Revenue

APPENDIX 2 PROBLEM 4-13 _____, Continued

Wages Expense

Rent Expense

Utilities Expense

Amortization Expense

Laundry Supplies Expense

Insurance Expense

Miscellaneous Expense

APPENDIX 2 PROBLEM 4-13 _____, Continued

End-of-Period Spreadsheet (Work Sheet)

	A	B	C	D	E	F	G	H	I	J	K
		Unadjusted Trial Balance		Adjustments		Adjusted Trial Balance		Income Statement		Balance Sheet	
	Account Title	Dr.	Cr.	Dr.	Cr.	Dr.	Cr.	Dr.	Cr.	Dr.	Cr.
1											
2											
3											
4											
5											
6											
7											
8											
9											
10											
11											
12											
13											
14											
15											
16											
17											
18											
19											
20											
21											
22											
23											
24											
25											
26											
27											
28											
29											
30											

APPENDIX 2 PROBLEM 4-13 ___ , Continued

2.   **JOURNAL**   PAGE 3

	DATE		DESCRIPTION	POST. REF.	DEBIT	CREDIT	
1			*Adjusting Entries*				1
2							2
3							3
4							4
5							5
6							6
7							7
8							8
9							9
10							10
11							11
12							12
13							13
14							14
15							15
16							16
17							17
18							18
19							19
20							20
21							21
22							22
23							23
24							24
25							25
26							26
27							27
28							28
29							29
30							30
31							31
32							32
33							33
34							34
35							35
36							36

APPENDIX 2 PROBLEM 4-13 ___, Continued

3.

Adjusted Trial Balance

APPENDIX 2 PROBLEM 4-13 ___, Continued

4.

Income Statement		

Statement of Owner's Equity		

APPENDIX 2 PROBLEM 4-13 ____, Continued

Balance Sheet

APPENDIX 2 PROBLEM 4-13 ___ , Concluded

5.

JOURNAL   PAGE

	DATE		DESCRIPTION	POST. REF.	DEBIT	CREDIT	
1			*Closing Entries*				1
2							2
3							3
4							4
5							5
6							6
7							7
8							8
9							9
10							10
11							11
12							12
13							13
14							14
15							15
16							16
17							17
18							18
19							19

6.

Post-Closing Trial Balance

This page not used.

APPENDIX 2 PROBLEM 4-14 _____

End-of-Period Spreadsheet (Work Sheet)

	Unadjusted Trial Balance		Adjustments		Adjusted Trial Balance		Income Statement		Balance Sheet	
Account Title	Dr.	Cr.	Dr.	Cr.	Dr.	Cr.	Dr.	Cr.	Dr.	Cr.
Cash	26,870									
Accounts Receivable	10,900									
Supplies	3,050									
Prepaid Insurance	4,800									
Building	312,000									
Accum. Depr.—Building		0								
Equipment	150,000									
Accum. Depr.—Equipment		0								
Land	50,000									
Accounts Payable		3,350								
Wages Payable										
Unearned Rent		2,700								
Young Lee, Capital		529,100								
Young Lee, Withdrawals	2,000									
Service Revenue		35,000								
Rent Revenue										
Wages Expense	5,000									
Supplies Expense										
Rent Expense	2,500									
Depreciation Expense										
Utilities Expense	1,650									
Insurance Expense										
Misc. Expense	1,380									
	570,150	570,150								

APPENDIX 2 PROBLEM 4-14 ___ , Continued

1.

JOURNAL   PAGE *26*

	DATE		DESCRIPTION	POST. REF.	DEBIT	CREDIT	
1			*Adjusting Entries*				1
2							2
3							3
4							4
5							5
6							6
7							7
8							8
9							9
10							10
11							11
12							12
13							13
14							14
15							15
16							16
17							17
18							18
19							19
20							20
21							21
22							22
23							23
24							24
25							25
26							26
27							27
28							28
29							29
30							30
31							31
32							32
33							33
34							34
35							35
36							36

APPENDIX 2 PROBLEM 4-14 ____, Continued

2.

Adjusted Trial Balance		

APPENDIX 2 PROBLEM 4-14 ___, Continued

3.

	Income Statement		

	Statement of Owner's Equity		

APPENDIX 2 PROBLEM 4-14 ____, Continued

Balance Sheet

APPENDIX 2 PROBLEM 4-14 ___ , Continued

4.

JOURNAL   PAGE *27*

	DATE		DESCRIPTION	POST. REF.	DEBIT	CREDIT	
1			*Closing Entries*				1
2							2
3							3
4							4
5							5
6							6
7							7
8							8
9							9
10							10
11							11
12							12
13							13
14							14
15							15
16							16
17							17
18							18
19							19
20							20
21							21
22							22
23							23
24							24
25							25
26							26
27							27
28							28
29							29
30							30
31							31
32							32
33							33
34							34
35							35
36							36

APPENDIX 2 PROBLEM 4-14 ___,Continued

1. and 4.

ACCOUNT   *Cash*   ACCOUNT NO.   *1010*

DATE		ITEM	POST. REF.	DEBIT	CREDIT	BALANCE
2012 Dec.	1	Balance	√			6,000.00 Dr.
	3		23		2,500.00	3,500.00 Dr.
	4		23	5,000.00		8,500.00 Dr.
	5		23		400.00	8,100.00 Dr.
	7		23	3,200.00		11,300.00 Dr.
	8		23	5,900.00		17,200.00 Dr.
	8		23		4,500.00	12,700.00 Dr.
	8		23	9,400.00		22,100.00 Dr.
	10		24		500.00	21,600.00 Dr.
	12		24		2,400.00	19,200.00 Dr.
	15		24	7,800.00		27,000.00 Dr.
	16		24		1,000.00	26,000.00 Dr.
	19		24		2,100.00	23,900.00 Dr.
	22		24		1,200.00	22,700.00 Dr.
	22		24	8,100.00		30,800.00 Dr.
	24		25		800.00	30,000.00 Dr.
	26		25		2,600.00	27,400.00 Dr.
	30		25		350.00	27,050.00 Dr.
	30		25		600.00	26,450.00 Dr.
	31		25		1,000.00	25,450.00 Dr.
	31		25	2,200.00		27,650.00 Dr.
	31		25		780.00	26,870.00 Dr.

APPENDIX 2 PROBLEM 4-14 ___ , Continued

ACCOUNT   *Accounts Receivable*   ACCOUNT NO.   *1020*

DATE		ITEM	POST. REF.	DEBIT	CREDIT	BALANCE
2012 Dec.	1	Balance	√			12,500.00 Dr.
	7		23		3,200.00	9,300.00 Dr.
	8		23		5,900.00	3,400.00 Dr.
	22		24	7,500.00		10,900.00 Dr.

ACCOUNT   *Supplies*   ACCOUNT NO.   *1030*

DATE		ITEM	POST. REF.	DEBIT	CREDIT	BALANCE
2012 Dec.	1	Balance	√			1,750.00 Dr.
	10		24	500.00		2,2500.0 Dr.
	27		25	800.00		3,050.00 Dr.

ACCOUNT   *Prepaid Insurance*   ACCOUNT NO.   *1040*

DATE		ITEM	POST. REF.	DEBIT	CREDIT	BALANCE
2012 Dec	1	Balance	√			3,600.00 Dr.
	22		24	1,200.00		4,800.00 Dr.

APPENDIX 2 PROBLEM 4-14___, Continued

ACCOUNT   *Building*   ACCOUNT NO.   *1050*

DATE		ITEM	POST. REF.	DEBIT	CREDIT	BALANCE
2012 Dec.	1	Balance	√			312, 000.00 Dr.

ACCOUNT   *Accumulated Amortization—Building*   ACCOUNT NO.   *1060*

DATE		ITEM	POST. REF.	DEBIT	CREDIT	BALANCE
2012 Dec.	1	Balance	√			0 Cr.

ACCOUNT   *Equipment*   ACCOUNT NO.   *1070*

DATE		ITEM	POST. REF.	DEBIT	CREDIT	BALANCE
2012 Dec.	1	Balance	√			147, 250.00 Dr.
	3		23	2,750.00		150,000.00 Dr.

ACCOUNT   *Accumulated Amortization—Equipment*   ACCOUNT NO.   *1080*

DATE		ITEM	POST. REF.	DEBIT	CREDIT	BALANCE
2012 Dec.	1	Balance	√			0 Cr.

APPENDIX 2 PROBLEM　4-14____,Continued

ACCOUNT　*Land*　　　　　　　　　　ACCOUNT NO.　*1090*

DATE		ITEM	POST. REF.	DEBIT	CREDIT	BALANCE
2012 Dec.	1	Balance	√			50,000.00 Dr.

ACCOUNT　*Accounts Payable*　　　　　　　ACCOUNT NO.　*2010*

DATE		ITEM	POST. REF.	DEBIT	CREDIT	BALANCE
2012 Dec.	1	Balance	√			6,300.00 Cr.
	3		23		2,750.00	9,050.00 Cr.
	8		23	4,500.00		4,550.00 Cr.
	19		24	2,100.00		2,450.00 Cr.
	31		25		900.00	3,350.00 Cr.

ACCOUNT　*Wages Payable*　　　　　　　ACCOUNT NO.　*2020*

DATE		ITEM	POST. REF.	DEBIT	CREDIT	BALANCE

ACCOUNT　*Unearned Rent*　　　　　　　ACCOUNT NO.　*2030*

DATE		ITEM	POST. REF.	DEBIT	CREDIT	BALANCE
2012 Dec.	1	Balance	√			2,700.00 Cr.

APPENDIX 2 PROBLEM 4-14___, Continued

ACCOUNT   *Young Lee, Capital*   ACCOUNT NO.   *3010*

DATE		ITEM	POST. REF.	DEBIT	CREDIT	BALANCE
2012 Dec.	1	Balance	√			524,100.00 Cr.
	4	23	23		5,000.00	529,100.00 Cr.

ACCOUNT   *Young Lee, Withdrawals*   ACCOUNT NO.   *3020*

DATE		ITEM	POST. REF.	DEBIT	CREDIT	BALANCE
2012 Dec.	16		24	1,000.00		1,000.00 Dr.
	31		25	1,000.00		2,000.00 Dr.

ACCOUNT   *Income Summary*   ACCOUNT NO.   *3030*

DATE	ITEM	POST. REF.	DEBIT	CREDIT	BALANCE

APPENDIX 2 PROBLEM 4-14___, Continued

ACCOUNT   *Service Revenue*   ACCOUNT NO.   *4010*

DATE		ITEM	POST. REF.	DEBIT	CREDIT	BALANCE
2012 Dec.	8		23		9,400.00	9,400.00 Cr.
	15		24		7,800.00	17,200.00 Cr.
	22		24		8,100.00	25,300.00 Cr.
	22		24		7,500.00	32,800.00 Cr.
	31		25		2,200.00	35,000.00 Cr.

ACCOUNT   *Rent Revenue*   ACCOUNT NO.   *4020*

DATE	ITEM	POST. REF.	DEBIT	CREDIT	BALANCE

ACCOUNT   *Wages Expense*   ACCOUNT NO.   *5010*

DATE		ITEM	POST. REF.	DEBIT	CREDIT	BALANCE
2012 Dec.	12		24	2,400.00		2,400.00 Dr.
	26		25	2,600.00		5,000.00 Dr.

APPENDIX 2 PROBLEM 4-14___ , Continued

ACCOUNT *Supplies Expense* ACCOUNT NO. *5020*

DATE		ITEM	POST. REF.	DEBIT	CREDIT	BALANCE

ACCOUNT *Rent Expense* ACCOUNT NO. *5030*

DATE		ITEM	POST. REF.	DEBIT	CREDIT	BALANCE
2012 Dec.	3		23	2,500.00		2,500.00 Dr.

ACCOUNT *Depreciation Expense* ACCOUNT NO. *5040*

DATE		ITEM	POST. REF.	DEBIT	CREDIT	BALANCE

APPENDIX 2 PROBLEM 4-14___ , Continued

ACCOUNT   *Utilities Expense*   ACCOUNT NO.   5050

DATE		ITEM	POST. REF.	DEBIT	CREDIT	BALANCE
2012 Dec.	5		24	400.00		400.00 Dr.
	30		25	350.00		750.00 Dr.
	31		25	900.00		1,650.00 Dr.

ACCOUNT   *Insurance Expense*   ACCOUNT NO.   5070

DATE		ITEM	POST. REF.	DEBIT	CREDIT	BALANCE

ACCOUNT   *Miscellaneous Expense*   ACCOUNT NO.   5090

DATE		ITEM	POST. REF.	DEBIT	CREDIT	BALANCE
2012 Dec.	30		25	600.00		600.00 Dr..
	31		25	780.00		1,380.00 Dr

APPENDIX 2 PROBLEM 4-14 ___ , Concluded

5.

Post-Closing Trial Balance		

This page not used.

APPENDIX 2 PROBLEM 4-15 _____

	A	B	C	D	E	F	G	H	I	J	K
1						End-of-Period Spreadsheet (Work Sheet)					
2											
3											
4			Unadjusted		Adjustments		Adjusted		Income		Balance
5			Trial Balance				Trial Balance		Statement		Sheet
6	Account Title	Dr.	Cr.	Dr.	Cr.	Dr.	Cr.	Dr.	Cr.	Dr.	Cr.
7											
8											
9											
10											
11											
12											
13											
14											
15											
16											
17											
18											
19											
20											
21											
22											
23											
24											
25											
26											
27											
28											
29											
30											

APPENDIX 2 PROBLEM 4-15 ___, Continued

2.

JOURNAL

	DATE		DESCRIPTION	POST. REF.	DEBIT	CREDIT	
1			*Adjusting Entries*				1
2							2
3							3
4							4
5							5
6							6
7							7
8							8
9							9
10							10
11							11
12							12
13							13
14							14
15							15
16							16
17							17
18							18
19							19
20							20

APPENDIX 2 PROBLEM 4-15 ___, Continued

3.

Adjusted Trial Balance		

APPENDIX 2 PROBLEM 4-15 ___ , Continued

4.

	Income Statement		

	Statement of Owner's Equity		

APPENDIX 2 PROBLEM 4-15 _____, Continued

Balance Sheet

APPENDIX 2 PROBLEM 4-15 ___ , Continued

1., 2., and 5.

ACCOUNT   *Cash*   ACCOUNT NO.   *1010*

DATE		ITEM	POST. REF.	DEBIT	CREDIT	BALANCE

ACCOUNT   *Supplies*   ACCOUNT NO.   *1030*

DATE		ITEM	POST. REF.	DEBIT	CREDIT	BALANCE

ACCOUNT   *Prepaid Insurance*   ACCOUNT NO.   *1040*

DATE		ITEM	POST. REF.	DEBIT	CREDIT	BALANCE

ACCOUNT   *Equipment*   ACCOUNT NO.   *1060*

DATE		ITEM	POST. REF.	DEBIT	CREDIT	BALANCE

ACCOUNT   *Accumulated Depreciation—Equipment*   ACCOUNT NO.   *1070*

DATE		ITEM	POST. REF.	DEBIT	CREDIT	BALANCE

APPENDIX 2 PROBLEM 4-15 ____ , Continued

ACCOUNT   *Trucks*   ACCOUNT NO.   *1080*

DATE		ITEM	POST. REF.	DEBIT	CREDIT	BALANCE

ACCOUNT   *Accumulated Depreciation—Trucks*   ACCOUNT NO.   *1090*

DATE		ITEM	POST. REF.	DEBIT	CREDIT	BALANCE

ACCOUNT   *Accounts Payable*   ACCOUNT NO.   *2010*

DATE		ITEM	POST. REF.	DEBIT	CREDIT	BALANCE

ACCOUNT   *Wages Payable*   ACCOUNT NO.   *2020*

DATE		ITEM	POST. REF.	DEBIT	CREDIT	BALANCE

ACCOUNT   _____ , *Capital*   ACCOUNT NO.   *3010*

DATE		ITEM	POST. REF.	DEBIT	CREDIT	BALANCE

ACCOUNT   _____ , *Withdrawals*   ACCOUNT NO.   *3020*

DATE		ITEM	POST. REF.	DEBIT	CREDIT	BALANCE

APPENDIX 2 PROBLEM 4-15 ___, Continued

ACCOUNT   *Income Summary*   ACCOUNT NO.   *3030*

DATE		ITEM	POST. REF.	DEBIT	CREDIT	BALANCE	

ACCOUNT   *Service Revenue*   ACCOUNT NO.   *4010*

DATE		ITEM	POST. REF.	DEBIT	CREDIT	BALANCE	

ACCOUNT   *Wages Expense*   ACCOUNT NO.   *5010*

DATE		ITEM	POST. REF.	DEBIT	CREDIT	BALANCE	

ACCOUNT   *Rent Expense*   ACCOUNT NO.   *5030*

DATE		ITEM	POST. REF.	DEBIT	CREDIT	BALANCE	

APPENDIX 2 PROBLEM 4-15 ___ , Continued

ACCOUNT *Depreciation Expense* ACCOUNT NO. *5040*

DATE		ITEM	POST. REF.	DEBIT	CREDIT	BALANCE	

ACCOUNT *Truck Expense* ACCOUNT NO. *5050*

DATE		ITEM	POST. REF.	DEBIT	CREDIT	BALANCE	

ACCOUNT *Miscellaneous Expense* ACCOUNT NO. *5090*

DATE		ITEM	POST. REF.	DEBIT	CREDIT	BALANCE	

APPENDIX 2 PROBLEM 4-15 ___, Concluded

5.

JOURNAL   PAGE *27*

	DATE		DESCRIPTION	POST. REF.	DEBIT	CREDIT	
1			*Closing Entries*				1
2							2
3							3
4							4
5							5
6							6
7							7
8							8
9							9
10							10
11							11
12							12
13							13
14							14
15							15
16							16
17							17
18							18
19							19
20							20

6.

Post-Closing Trial Balance

APPENDIX 2 PROBLEM 4-16 ____

End-of-Period Spreadsheet (Work Sheet)

Account Title	Unadjusted Trial Balance		Adjustments		Adjusted Trial Balance		Income Statement		Balance Sheet	
	Dr.	Cr.	Dr.	Cr.	Dr.	Cr.	Dr.	Cr.	Dr.	Cr.
1										
2										
3										
4										
5										
6										
7										
8										
9										
10										
11										
12										
13										
14										
15										
16										
17										
18										
19										
20										
21										
22										
23										
24										
25										
26										
27										
28										
29										
30										
31										
32										

APPENDIX 2 PROBLEM 4-16 ___ Continued

1.   **JOURNAL**   PAGE *1*

	DATE		DESCRIPTION	POST. REF.	DEBIT	CREDIT	
1							1
2							2
3							3
4							4
5							5
6							6
7							7
8							8
9							9
10							10
11							11
12							12
13							13
14							14
15							15
16							16
17							17
18							18
19							19
20							20
21							21
22							22
23							23
24							24
25							25
26							26
27							27
28							28
29							29
30							30
31							31
32							32
33							33
34							34
35							35
36							36

APPENDIX 2 PROBLEM 4-16 ___, Continued

2., 5., and 8.

ACCOUNT   *Cash*   ACCOUNT NO.   *1010*

DATE		ITEM	POST. REF.	DEBIT	CREDIT	BALANCE

ACCOUNT   *Accounts Receivable*   ACCOUNT NO.   *1020*

DATE		ITEM	POST. REF.	DEBIT	CREDIT	BALANCE

APPENDIX 2 PROBLEM 4-16 ___ , Continued

ACCOUNT   *Supplies*   ACCOUNT NO.   *1040*

DATE		ITEM	POST. REF.	DEBIT	CREDIT	BALANCE	

ACCOUNT   *Prepaid Rent*   ACCOUNT NO.   *1050*

DATE		ITEM	POST. REF.	DEBIT	CREDIT	BALANCE	

ACCOUNT   *Prepaid Insurance*   ACCOUNT NO.   *1060*

DATE		ITEM	POST. REF.	DEBIT	CREDIT	BALANCE	

ACCOUNT   *Office Equipment*   ACCOUNT NO.   *1080*

DATE		ITEM	POST. REF.	DEBIT	CREDIT	BALANCE	

ACCOUNT   *Accumulated Depreciation*   ACCOUNT NO.   *1090*

DATE		ITEM	POST. REF.	DEBIT	CREDIT	BALANCE	

APPENDIX 2 PROBLEM 4-16 ___ , Continued

ACCOUNT   *Accounts Payable*   ACCOUNT NO. *2010*

DATE		ITEM	POST. REF.	DEBIT	CREDIT	BALANCE

ACCOUNT   *Unearned Fees*   ACCOUNT NO. *2030*

DATE		ITEM	POST. REF.	DEBIT	CREDIT	BALANCE

ACCOUNT _____ *, Capital*   ACCOUNT NO. *3010*

DATE		ITEM	POST. REF.	DEBIT	CREDIT	BALANCE

ACCOUNT _____ *, Withdrawals*   ACCOUNT NO. *3020*

DATE		ITEM	POST. REF.	DEBIT	CREDIT	BALANCE

APPENDIX 2 PROBLEM 4-16 ___ , Continued

ACCOUNT   *Income Summary*   ACCOUNT NO.   3030

DATE	ITEM	POST. REF.	DEBIT	CREDIT	BALANCE

ACCOUNT   *Fees Earned*   ACCOUNT NO.   4010

DATE	ITEM	POST. REF.	DEBIT	CREDIT	BALANCE

ACCOUNT   *Rent Expense*   ACCOUNT NO.   5020

DATE	ITEM	POST. REF.	DEBIT	CREDIT	BALANCE

APPENDIX 2 PROBLEM 4-16 ___ , Continued

ACCOUNT   *Supplies Expense*   ACCOUNT NO.   *5030*

DATE		ITEM	POST. REF.	DEBIT	CREDIT	BALANCE

ACCOUNT   *Depreciation Expense*   ACCOUNT NO.   *5040*

DATE		ITEM	POST. REF.	DEBIT	CREDIT	BALANCE

ACCOUNT   *Insurance Expense*   ACCOUNT NO.   *5050*

DATE		ITEM	POST. REF.	DEBIT	CREDIT	BALANCE

ACCOUNT   *Miscellaneous Expense*   ACCOUNT NO.   *5090*

DATE		ITEM	POST. REF.	DEBIT	CREDIT	BALANCE

APPENDIX 2 PROBLEM 4-16 ___ , Continued

3.

	Unadjusted Trial Balance		

APPENDIX 2 PROBLEM 4-16 ___ , Continued

5.   **JOURNAL**   PAGE 3

	DATE		DESCRIPTION	POST. REF.	DEBIT	CREDIT	
1			*Adjusting Entries*				1
2							2
3							3
4							4
5							5
6							6
7							7
8							8
9							9
10							10
11							11
12							12
13							13
14							14
15							15
16							16
17							17
18							18
19							19
20							20
21							21
22							22
23							23
24							24

APPENDIX 2 PROBLEM 4-16 ___ , Continued

6.

Adjusted Trial Balance		

APPENDIX 2 PROBLEM 4-16 ___ , Continued

7.

Income Statement		

Statement of Owner's Equity		

APPENDIX 2 PROBLEM 4-16 ____, Continued

Balance Sheet

APPENDIX 2 PROBLEM 4-16 ___ , Concluded

8.   **JOURNAL**   PAGE *4*

	DATE	DESCRIPTION	POST. REF.	DEBIT	CREDIT	
1		*Closing Entries*				1
2						2
3						3
4						4
5						5
6						6
7						7
8						8
9						9
10						10
11						11
12						12
13						13
14						14
15						15
16						16
17						17
18						18

9.

Post-Closing Trial Balance

This page not used.

1. Optional (Appendix)

End-of-Period Spreadsheet (Work Sheet)

	A	B	C	D	E	F	G	H	I	J	K
		Unadjusted Trial Balance		Adjustments		Adjusted Trial Balance		Income Statement		Balance Sheet	
	Account Title	Dr.	Cr.	Dr.	Cr.	Dr.	Cr.	Dr.	Cr.	Dr.	Cr.
7											
8											
9											
10											
11											
12											
13											
14											
15											
16											
17											
18											
19											
20											
21											
22											
23											
24											
25											
26											
27											
28											
29											
30											
31											
32											

CONTINUING PROBLEM, Continued

2.

Income Statement

Statement of Owner's Equity

Balance Sheet

CONTINUING PROBLEM, Continued

3. Note: Use the general ledger accounts provided in Chapter 3.

JOURNAL

	DATE		DESCRIPTION	POST. REF.	DEBIT	CREDIT	
1			*Closing Entries*				1
2							2
3							3
4							4
5							5
6							6
7							7
8							8
9							9
10							10
11							11
12							12
13							13
14							14
15							15
16							16
17							17
18							18
19							19
20							20
21							21
22							22
23							23
24							24
25							25
26							26
27							27
28							28
29							29
30							30
31							31
32							32
33							33
34							34

INUING PROBLEM, Continued

UNT *Cash* ACCOUNT NO. *1010*

TE	ITEM	POST. REF.	DEBIT	CREDIT	BALANCE	

UNT *Accounts Receivable* ACCOUNT NO. *1020*

TE	ITEM	POST. REF.	DEBIT	CREDIT	BALANCE	

CONTINUING PROBLEM, Continued

ACCOUNT *Prepaid Insurance*   ACCOUNT NO.   *1030*

DATE		ITEM	POST. REF.	DEBIT	CREDIT	BALANCE

ACCOUNT *Supplies*   ACCOUNT NO.   *1040*

DATE		ITEM	POST. REF.	DEBIT	CREDIT	BALANCE

ACCOUNT *Office Equipment*   ACCOUNT NO.   *1070*

DATE		ITEM	POST. REF.	DEBIT	CREDIT	BALANCE

ACCOUNT *Accumulated Depreciation—Office Equipment*   ACCOUNT NO.   *1080*

DATE		ITEM	POST. REF.	DEBIT	CREDIT	BALANCE

ACCOUNT *Accounts Payable*   ACCOUNT NO.   *2010*

DATE		ITEM	POST. REF.	DEBIT	CREDIT	BALANCE

NUING PROBLEM, Continued

UNT   *Wages Payable*   ACCOUNT NO.   *2020*

TE	ITEM	POST. REF.	DEBIT	CREDIT	BALANCE	

UNT   *Unearned Revenue*   ACCOUNT NO.   *2030*

TE	ITEM	POST. REF.	DEBIT	CREDIT	BALANCE	

UNT   _____ *, Capital*   ACCOUNT NO.   *3010*

TE	ITEM	POST. REF.	DEBIT	CREDIT	BALANCE	

UNT   _____ *, Withdrawals*   ACCOUNT NO.   *3020*

TE	ITEM	POST. REF.	DEBIT	CREDIT	BALANCE	

CONTINUING PROBLEM, Continued

ACCOUNT   *Income Summary*   ACCOUNT NO.   *3030*

DATE		ITEM	POST. REF.	DEBIT	CREDIT	BALANCE	

ACCOUNT   *Fees Earned*   ACCOUNT NO.   *4010*

DATE		ITEM	POST. REF.	DEBIT	CREDIT	BALANCE	

ACCOUNT   *Music Expense*   ACCOUNT NO.   *5040*

DATE		ITEM	POST. REF.	DEBIT	CREDIT	BALANCE	

ACCOUNT   *Advertising Expense*   ACCOUNT NO.   *5050*

DATE		ITEM	POST. REF.	DEBIT	CREDIT	BALANCE	

NUING PROBLEM, Continued

JNT *Supplies Expense*   ACCOUNT NO.   *5060*

E	ITEM	POST. REF.	DEBIT	CREDIT	BALANCE	

JNT *Depreciation Expense*   ACCOUNT NO.   *5080*

E	ITEM	POST. REF.	DEBIT	CREDIT	BALANCE	

JNT *Insurance Expense*   ACCOUNT NO.   *5090*

E	ITEM	POST. REF.	DEBIT	CREDIT	BALANCE	

JNT *Wage Expense*   ACCOUNT NO.   *5100*

E	ITEM	POST. REF.	DEBIT	CREDIT	BALANCE	

CONTINUING PROBLEM, Concluded

4.

Post-Closing Trial Balance		

REHENSIVE PROBLEM 1

2.

JOURNAL

PAGE 5

DATE	DESCRIPTION	POST. REF.	DEBIT	CREDIT	
					1
					2
					3
					4
					5
					6
					7
					8
					9
					10
					11
					12
					13
					14
					15
					16
					17
					18
					19
					20
					21
					22
					23
					24
					25
					26
					27
					28
					29
					30
					31
					32
					33
					34
					35

COMPREHENSIVE PROBLEM 1, Continued

1., 2., 6., and 9.

ACCOUNT　*Cash*　　　　　　　　　　　　　　ACCOUNT NO.　*1010*

DATE		ITEM	POST. REF.	DEBIT	CREDIT	BALANCE

ACCOUNT　*Accounts Receivable*　　　　　　　　ACCOUNT NO.　*1020*

DATE		ITEM	POST. REF.	DEBIT	CREDIT	BALANCE

ACCOUNT　*Supplies*　　　　　　　　　　　　　ACCOUNT NO.　*1040*

DATE		ITEM	POST. REF.	DEBIT	CREDIT	BALANCE

REHENSIVE PROBLEM 1, Continued

UNT *Prepaid Rent* ACCOUNT NO. *1050*

TE	ITEM	POST. REF.	DEBIT	CREDIT	BALANCE	

UNT *Office Equipment* ACCOUNT NO. *1080*

TE	ITEM	POST. REF.	DEBIT	CREDIT	BALANCE	

UNT *Accumulated Depreciation* ACCOUNT NO. *1090*

TE	ITEM	POST. REF.	DEBIT	CREDIT	BALANCE	

UNT *Accounts Payable* ACCOUNT NO. *2010*

TE	ITEM	POST. REF.	DEBIT	CREDIT	BALANCE	

COMPREHENSIVE PROBLEM 1, Continued

ACCOUNT   *Salaries Payable*   ACCOUNT NO.   *2020*

DATE		ITEM	POST. REF.	DEBIT	CREDIT	BALANCE

ACCOUNT   *Unearned Fees*   ACCOUNT NO.   *2030*

DATE		ITEM	POST. REF.	DEBIT	CREDIT	BALANCE

ACCOUNT   *Kelly Pitney, Capital*   ACCOUNT NO.   *3010*

DATE		ITEM	POST. REF.	DEBIT	CREDIT	BALANCE

ACCOUNT   *Kelly Pitney, Withdrawals*   ACCOUNT NO.   *3020*

DATE		ITEM	POST. REF.	DEBIT	CREDIT	BALANCE

EHENSIVE PROBLEM 1, Continued

NT *Income Summary* ACCOUNT NO. *3030*

E	ITEM	POST. REF.	DEBIT	CREDIT	BALANCE	

NT *Fees Earned* ACCOUNT NO. *4010*

E	ITEM	POST. REF.	DEBIT	CREDIT	BALANCE	

NT *Salary Expense* ACCOUNT NO. *5010*

E	ITEM	POST. REF.	DEBIT	CREDIT	BALANCE	

NT *Rent Expense* ACCOUNT NO. *5020*

E	ITEM	POST. REF.	DEBIT	CREDIT	BALANCE	

COMPREHENSIVE PROBLEM 1, Continued

ACCOUNT   *Supplies Expense*   ACCOUNT NO.   *5030*

DATE		ITEM	POST. REF.	DEBIT	CREDIT	BALANCE

ACCOUNT   *Depreciation Expense*   ACCOUNT NO.   *5040*

DATE		ITEM	POST. REF.	DEBIT	CREDIT	BALANCE

ACCOUNT   *Utilities Expense*   ACCOUNT NO.   *5090*

DATE		ITEM	POST. REF.	DEBIT	CREDIT	BALANCE

ACCOUNT   *Miscellaneous Expense*   ACCOUNT NO.   *5050*

DATE		ITEM	POST. REF.	DEBIT	CREDIT	BALANCE

COMPREHENSIVE PROBLEM 1, Continued

	Unadjusted Trial Balance		

COMPREHENSIVE PROBLEM 1, Continued

5. Optional (Appendix)

End-of-Period Spreadsheet (Work Sheet)

	Unadjusted Trial Balance		Adjustments		Adjusted Trial Balance		Income Statement		Balance Sheet	
Account Title	Dr.	Cr.	Dr.	Cr.	Dr.	Cr.	Dr.	Cr.	Dr.	Cr.

REHENSIVE PROBLEM 1, Continued

JOURNAL

DATE		DESCRIPTION	POST. REF.	DEBIT	CREDIT	
		Adjusting Entries				1
						2
						3
						4
						5
						6
						7
						8
						9
						10
						11
						12
						13
						14
						15
						16
						17
						18
						19
						20

COMPREHENSIVE PROBLEM 1, Continued

7.

Adjusted Trial Balance		

REHENSIVE PROBLEM 1, Continued

Income Statement

Statement of Owner's Equity

COMPREHENSIVE PROBLEM 1, Continued

Balance Sheet

REHENSIVE PROBLEM 1, Continued

JOURNAL

DATE	DESCRIPTION	POST. REF.	DEBIT	CREDIT	
	Closing Entries				1
					2
					3
					4
					5
					6
					7
					8
					9
					10
					11
					12
					13

COMPREHENSIVE PROBLEM 1, Concluded

10.

	Post-Closing Trial Balance		

EXERCISE 5-1

a. _____

b. _____

c. _____

_____

EXERCISE 5-2

_____

EXERCISE 5-3

Balance Sheet Accounts		Income Statement Accounts	
Acct #	**Account Name**	**Acct #**	**Account Name**

EXERCISE 5-3 Continued

Balance Sheet Accounts	
Acct #	Account Name

Income Statement Accounts	
Acct #	Account Name

EXERCISE 5-4

a. _____

_____

b. _____

_____

EXERCISE 5-5

_____

_____

_____

_____

_____

_____

_____

_____

_____

_____

EXERCISE 5-6

(1) _____

_____

_____

(2) _____

_____

_____

(3) _____

_____

_____

(4) _____

_____

_____

EXERCISE 5-7

JOURNAL   PAGE

	DATE		DESCRIPTION	POST. REF.	DEBIT	CREDIT	
1							1
2							2
3							3
4							4
5							5
6							6
7							7
8							8
9							9
10							10

EXERCISE 5-8

JOURNAL   PAGE

	DATE	DESCRIPTION	POST. REF.	DEBIT	CREDIT	
1						1
2						2
3						3
4						4
5						5
6						6
7						7
8						8
9						9
10						10
11						11
12						12
13						13
14						14
15						15
16						16

EXERCISE 5-9

	Merchandise	Freight Paid by Seller		Returns and Allowances	Amount to be Paid in Full
a.	$15,000	—	FOB destination, n/30	$800	$ _____
b.	10,000	$400	FOB shipping point, 2/10, n/30	1,200	$ _____
c.	$8,250	—	FOB shipping point, 1/10, n/30	$750	$ _____
d.	2,900	125	FOB shipping point, 2/10, n/30	400	$ _____
e.	3,850	—	FOB destination, 2/10, n/30	—	$ _____

EXERCISE 5-10

JOURNAL

	DATE		DESCRIPTION	POST. REF.	DEBIT	CREDIT	
1							1
2							2
3							3
4							4
5							5
6							6
7							7
8							8
9							9
10							10
11							11
12							12
13							13
14							14
15							15
16							16
17							17
18							18
19							19
20							20

EXERCISE 5-11

EXERCISE 5-12

a. _____

b. _____

JOURNAL   PAGE

	DATE		DESCRIPTION	POST. REF.	DEBIT	CREDIT	
1							1
2							2
3							3
4							4
5							5
6							6

EXERCISE 5-13

(1) _____

_____

(2) _____

_____

(3) _____

_____

(4) _____

_____

(5) _____

_____

EXERCISE 5-14

a. Amount of the sale: _____

b. Amount debited to Accounts Receivable: _____

c. Amount of the discount for early payment: _____

d. Amount due within the discount period: _____

EXERCISE 5-15

		JOURNAL				PAGE	
	DATE	DESCRIPTION	POST. REF.	DEBIT	CREDIT		
1							1
2							2
3							3
4							4
5							5
6							6
7							7
8							8
9							9
10							10
11							11
12							12
13							13
14							14
15							15
16							16
17							17
18							18

EXERCISE 5-16

JOURNAL   PAGE

	DATE		DESCRIPTION	POST. REF.	DEBIT	CREDIT	
1							1
2							2
3							3
4							4
5							5
6							6
7							7
8							8
9							9
10							10
11							11
12							12

EXERCISE 5-17

		Debit	Credit
a.	Cost of Goods Sold	_____	_____
b.	Delivery Expense	_____	_____
c.	Inventory	_____	_____
d.	Sales	_____	_____
e.	Sales Discounts	_____	_____
f.	Sales Returns and Allowances	_____	_____
g.	Provincial Sales Tax Payable	_____	_____

EXERCISE 5-18

JOURNAL   PAGE

	DATE		DESCRIPTION	POST. REF.	DEBIT	CREDIT	
1							1
2							2
3							3
4							4
5							5
6							6

EXERCISE 5-19

a. Net sales: _____

b. Gross profit: _____

EXERCISE 5-20

1. Advertising expense: _____

2. Depreciation expense on store equipment: _____

3. Insurance expense on office equipment: _____

4. Interest expense on notes payable: _____

5. Rent expense on office building: _____

6. Salaries of office personnel: _____

7. Salary of sales manager: _____

8. Sales supplies used: _____

EXERCISE 5-21

	Income Statement		

EXERCISE 5-22

(Optional)

Income Statement

EXERCISE 5-23

a. _____

b. _____

c. _____

d. _____

e. _____

f. _____

g. _____

h. _____

EXERCISE 5-24

a.

Income Statement

b. _____

_____

_____

_____

_____

_____

EXERCISE 5-25

a. _____
_____
_____
_____
_____

b. _____
_____
_____
_____
_____

c. _____
_____
_____
_____
_____

EXERCISE 5-26

a. Accounts Payable: _____

b. Advertising Expense: _____

c. Cost of Goods Sold: _____

d. Inventory: _____

e. Sales: _____

f. Sales Discounts: _____

g. Sales Returns and Allowances: _____

h. Supplies: _____

i. Supplies Expense: _____

j. Talia Greenly, Withdrawal: _____

k. Wages Payable: _____

EXERCISE 5-27

JOURNAL

	DATE		DESCRIPTION	POST. REF.	DEBIT	CREDIT	
1							1
2							2
3							3
4							4
5							5
6							6
7							7
8							8
9							9
10							10
11							11
12							12
13							13
14							14
15							15
16							16
17							17
18							18
19							19
20							20
21							21
22							22
23							23

EXERCISE 5-28

JOURNAL

	DATE		DESCRIPTION	POST. REF.	DEBIT	CREDIT	
1							1
2							2
3							3
4							4
5							5
6							6
7							7
8							8
9							9
10							10
11							11
12							12
13							13
14							14
15							15
16							16
17							17
18							18
19							19
20							20

APPENDIX 1—EXERCISE 5-29

a. Purchases − (X + Y) = Net purchases

_____

b. Net purchases + X = Cost of goods purchased

_____

c. Inventory (beginning) + Cost of goods purchased = X

_____

d. Goods available for sale − X = Cost of goods sold

_____

APPENDIX 1—EXERCISE 5-30

a. _____

APPENDIX 1—EXERCISE 5-30, Concluded

b. _____

APPENDIX 1—EXERCISE 5-31

1. _____
2. _____
3. _____
4. _____
5. _____
6. _____
7. _____
8. _____
9. _____
10._____

APPENDIX 1—EXERCISE 5-32

a. _____
b. _____
c. _____
d. _____
e. _____
f. _____
g. _____

APPENDIX 1—EXERCISE 5-33

JOURNAL

	DATE		DESCRIPTION	POST. REF.	DEBIT	CREDIT	
1							1
2							2
3							3
4							4
5							5
6							6
7							7
8							8
9							9
10							10
11							11
12							12
13							13
14							14
15							15
16							16
17							17
18							18
19							19
20							20
21							21
22							22

APPENDIX 1—EXERCISE 5-34

JOURNAL

	DATE		DESCRIPTION	POST. REF.	DEBIT	CREDIT	
1							1
2							2
3							3
4							4
5							5
6							6
7							7
8							8
9							9
10							10
11							11
12							12
13							13
14							14
15							15
16							16
17							17
18							18
19							19
20							20
21							21
22							22
23							23
24							24
25							25

APPENDIX 1—EXERCISE 5-35

APPENDIX 1—EXERCISE 5-36

APPENDIX 1—EXERCISE 5-37

_____
_____
_____
_____
_____
_____
_____
_____
_____
_____
_____

(Optional)

APPENDIX 1—EXERCISE 5-38

JOURNAL   PAGE

	DATE		DESCRIPTION	POST. REF.	DEBIT	CREDIT	
1							1
2							2
3							3
4							4
5							5
6							6
7							7
8							8
9							9
10							10
11							11
12							12
13							13
14							14
15							15
16							16
17							17
18							18
19							19
20							20
21							21
22							22
23							23
24							24
25							25

APPENDIX 1—EXERCISE 5-39

JOURNAL   PAGE

	DATE		DESCRIPTION	POST. REF.	DEBIT	CREDIT	
1							1
2							2
3							3
4							4
5							5
6							6
7							7
8							8
9							9
10							10
11							11
12							12
13							13
14							14
15							15
16							16
17							17
18							18
19							19
20							20
21							21
22							22
23							23
24							24
25							25

APPENDIX 2—EXERCISE 5-40

a. _____

b. _____

c. _____

d. _____

APPENDIX 2—EXERCISE 5-41

a. _____

b. _____

c. _____

d. _____

APPENDIX 2—EXERCISE 5-42

a. _____

b. _____

c. _____

d. _____

APPENDIX 2—EXERCISE 5-43

Choose to complete a., b., or c.

JOURNAL   PAGE

	DATE		DESCRIPTION	POST. REF.	DEBIT	CREDIT	
1							1
2							2
3							3
4							4
5							5

APPENDIX 2—EXERCISE 5-44

Choose to complete a., b., or c.

JOURNAL   PAGE

	DATE		DESCRIPTION	POST. REF.	DEBIT	CREDIT	
1							1
2							2
3							3
4							4
5							5
6							6
7							7
8							8
9							9
10							10
11							11
12							12
13							13
14							14
15							15
16							16
17							17
18							18
19							19
20							20

APPENDIX 2—EXERCISE 5-45
Choose to complete a., b., or c.

1.

	JOURNAL				PAGE

	DATE		DESCRIPTION	POST. REF.	DEBIT	CREDIT	
1							1
2							2
3							3
4							4
5							5
6							6
7							7
8							8

2.

	JOURNAL				PAGE

	DATE		DESCRIPTION	POST. REF.	DEBIT	CREDIT	
1							1
2							2
3							3
4							4
5							5

APPENDIX 1—EXERCISE 5-45 Concluded

3.

JOURNAL   PAGE

	DATE		DESCRIPTION	POST. REF.	DEBIT	CREDIT	
1							1
2							2
3							3
4							4
5							5
6							6
7							7
8							8
9							9
10							10
11							11
12							12
13							13

_____

_____

_____

_____

_____

APPENDIX 2—EXERCISE 5-46

Choose to complete a., b., or c.

1. _____

2. _____

3. _____

PROBLEM 5-1 ___

JOURNAL   PAGE

	DATE		DESCRIPTION	POST. REF.	DEBIT	CREDIT	
1							1
2							2
3							3
4							4
5							5
6							6
7							7
8							8
9							9
10							10
11							11
12							12
13							13
14							14
15							15
16							16
17							17
18							18
19							19
20							20
21							21
22							22
23							23
24							24
25							25
26							26
27							27
28							28
29							29
30							30
31							31
32							32
33							33
34							34
35							35
36							36

This page not used.

PROBLEM 5-2 ___

JOURNAL

	DATE		DESCRIPTION	POST. REF.	DEBIT	CREDIT	
1							1
2							2
3							3
4							4
5							5
6							6
7							7
8							8
9							9
10							10
11							11
12							12
13							13
14							14
15							15
16							16
17							17
18							18
19							19
20							20
21							21
22							22
23							23
24							24
25							25
26							26
27							27
28							28
29							29
30							30
31							31
32							32
33							33
34							34
35							35
36							36

This page not used.

PROBLEM 5-3 ___

JOURNAL

PAGE

	DATE		DESCRIPTION	POST. REF.	DEBIT	CREDIT	
1							1
2							2
3							3
4							4
5							5
6							6
7							7
8							8
9							9
10							10
11							11
12							12
13							13
14							14
15							15
16							16
17							17
18							18
19							19
20							20
21							21
22							22
23							23
24							24
25							25
26							26
27							27
28							28
29							29
30							30
31							31
32							32
33							33
34							34
35							35
36							36

PROBLEM 5-3___ , Concluded

JOURNAL   PAGE

	DATE		DESCRIPTION	POST. REF.	DEBIT	CREDIT	
1							1
2							2
3							3
4							4
5							5
6							6
7							7
8							8
9							9
10							10
11							11
12							12
13							13
14							14
15							15
16							16
17							17
18							18
19							19
20							20
21							21
22							22
23							23
24							24
25							25
26							26
27							27
28							28
29							29
30							30
31							31
32							32
33							33
34							34
35							35
36							36

PROBLEM 5-4 ___

JOURNAL   PAGE

	DATE		DESCRIPTION	POST. REF.	DEBIT	CREDIT	
1							1
2							2
3							3
4							4
5							5
6							6
7							7
8							8
9							9
10							10
11							11
12							12
13							13
14							14
15							15
16							16
17							17
18							18
19							19
20							20
21							21
22							22
23							23
24							24
25							25
26							26
27							27
28							28
29							29
30							30
31							31
32							32
33							33
34							34
35							35
36							36

PROBLEM 5-4___, Concluded

JOURNAL

	DATE		DESCRIPTION	POST. REF.	DEBIT	CREDIT	
1							1
2							2
3							3
4							4
5							5
6							6
7							7
8							8
9							9
10							10
11							11
12							12
13							13
14							14
15							15
16							16
17							17
18							18
19							19
20							20
21							21
22							22
23							23
24							24
25							25
26							26
27							27
28							28
29							29
30							30
31							31
32							32
33							33
34							34
35							35
36							36

PROBLEM 5-5 ___

JOURNAL   PAGE

	DATE		DESCRIPTION	POST. REF.	DEBIT	CREDIT	
1							1
2							2
3							3
4							4
5							5
6							6
7							7
8							8
9							9
10							10
11							11
12							12
13							13
14							14
15							15
16							16
17							17
18							18
19							19
20							20
21							21
22							22
23							23
24							24
25							25
26							26
27							27
28							28
29							29
30							30
31							31
32							32
33							33
34							34
35							35
36							36

This page not used.

PROBLEM 5-6___

	DATE		DESCRIPTION	POST. REF.	DEBIT	CREDIT	
1							1
2							2
3							3
4							4
5							5
6							6
7							7
8							8
9							9
10							10
11							11
12							12
13							13
14							14
15							15
16							16
17							17
18							18
19							19
20							20
21							21
22							22
23							23
24							24
25							25
26							26
27							27
28							28
29							29
30							30
31							31
32							32
33							33
34							34
35							35
36							36

JOURNAL   PAGE

PROBLEM 5-6___, Concluded

JOURNAL   PAGE

	DATE		DESCRIPTION	POST. REF.	DEBIT	CREDIT	
1							1
2							2
3							3
4							4
5							5
6							6
7							7
8							8
9							9
10							10
11							11
12							12
13							13
14							14
15							15
16							16
17							17
18							18
19							19
20							20
21							21
22							22
23							23
24							24
25							25
26							26
27							27
28							28
29							29
30							30
31							31
32							32
33							33
34							34
35							35
36							36

PROBLEM 5-7 ___

1.

JOURNAL

PAGE _____

	DATE		DESCRIPTION	POST. REF.	DEBIT	CREDIT	
1							1
2							2
3							3
4							4
5							5
6							6
7							7
8							8
9							9
10							10
11							11
12							12
13							13
14							14
15							15
16							16
17							17
18							18
19							19
20							20
21							21
22							22
23							23
24							24
25							25
26							26
27							27
28							28
29							29
30							30
31							31
32							32
33							33
34							34
35							35
36							36

PROBLEM 5-7 ___, Concluded

2.

JOURNAL

	DATE		DESCRIPTION	POST. REF.	DEBIT	CREDIT	
1							1
2							2
3							3
4							4
5							5
6							6
7							7
8							8
9							9
10							10
11							11
12							12
13							13
14							14
15							15
16							16
17							17
18							18
19							19
20							20
21							21
22							22
23							23
24							24
25							25
26							26
27							27
28							28
29							29
30							30
31							31
32							32
33							33
34							34
35							35
36							36

PROBLEM 5-8___

JOURNAL

	DATE		DESCRIPTION	POST. REF.	DEBIT	CREDIT	
1							1
2							2
3							3
4							4
5							5
6							6
7							7
8							8
9							9
10							10
11							11
12							12
13							13
14							14
15							15
16							16
17							17
18							18
19							19
20							20
21							21
22							22
23							23
24							24
25							25
26							26
27							27
28							28
29							29
30							30
31							31
32							32
33							33
34							34
35							35
36							36

PROBLEM 5-8___, Concluded

JOURNAL   PAGE

	DATE		DESCRIPTION	POST. REF.	DEBIT	CREDIT	
1							1
2							2
3							3
4							4
5							5
6							6
7							7
8							8
9							9
10							10
11							11
12							12
13							13
14							14
15							15
16							16
17							17
18							18
19							19
20							20
21							21
22							22
23							23
24							24
25							25
26							26
27							27
28							28
29							29
30							30
31							31
32							32
33							33
34							34
35							35
36							36

PROBLEM 5-9 ___

1.

	Income Statement			

2.

	Statement of Owner's Equity		

PROBLEM 5-9 ___, Continued

3.

Balance Sheet			

PROBLEM 5-9 ___ , Concluded

4. _____

_____

_____

_____

_____

_____

_____

_____

_____

_____

_____

This page not used.

PROBLEM 5-10 ___

1.

	Income Statement		

PROBLEM 5-10 ___, Concluded

2.

JOURNAL

PAGE

	DATE		DESCRIPTION	POST. REF.	DEBIT	CREDIT	
1							1
2							2
3							3
4							4
5							5
6							6
7							7
8							8
9							9
10							10
11							11
12							12
13							13
14							14
15							15
16							16
17							17
18							18
19							19
20							20
21							21
22							22
23							23
24							24
25							25
26							26
27							27
28							28
29							29
30							30
31							31
32							32
33							33
34							34
35							35
36							36

APPENDIX 1—PROBLEM 5-11 ___

JOURNAL

	DATE		DESCRIPTION	POST. REF.	DEBIT	CREDIT	
1							1
2							2
3							3
4							4
5							5
6							6
7							7
8							8
9							9
10							10
11							11
12							12
13							13
14							14
15							15
16							16
17							17
18							18
19							19
20							20
21							21
22							22
23							23
24							24
25							25
26							26
27							27
28							28
29							29
30							30
31							31
32							32
33							33
34							34
35							35
36							36

This page not used.

APPENDIX 1—PROBLEM 5-12 ___

JOURNAL   PAGE

	DATE		DESCRIPTION	POST. REF.	DEBIT	CREDIT	
1							1
2							2
3							3
4							4
5							5
6							6
7							7
8							8
9							9
10							10
11							11
12							12
13							13
14							14
15							15
16							16
17							17
18							18
19							19
20							20
21							21
22							22
23							23
24							24
25							25
26							26
27							27
28							28
29							29
30							30
31							31
32							32
33							33
34							34
35							35
36							36

This page not used.

APPENDIX 1—PROBLEM 5-13 ___

1.

JOURNAL

	DATE		DESCRIPTION	POST. REF.	DEBIT	CREDIT	
1							1
2							2
3							3
4							4
5							5
6							6
7							7
8							8
9							9
10							10
11							11
12							12
13							13
14							14
15							15
16							16
17							17
18							18
19							19
20							20
21							21
22							22
23							23
24							24
25							25
26							26
27							27
28							28
29							29
30							30
31							31
32							32
33							33
34							34
35							35
36							36

This page not used.

APPENDIX 2—PROBLEM 5-14 ___

1.

_____

_____

_____

2.

_____

Income Statement

APPENDIX 2—PROBLEM 5-14 ___, Continued

2.

Income Statement (Continued)			

APPENDIX 2—PROBLEM 5-14 ___, Concluded

3.

JOURNAL

	DATE		DESCRIPTION	POST. REF.	DEBIT	CREDIT	
1							1
2							2
3							3
4							4
5							5
6							6
7							7
8							8
9							9
10							10
11							11
12							12
13							13
14							14
15							15
16							16
17							17
18							18
19							19
20							20
21							21
22							22
23							23
24							24
25							25
26							26
27							27
28							28
29							29
30							30
31							31
32							32
33							33
34							34
35							35
36							36

This page not used.

APPENDIX 2—PROBLEM 5-15 ___
Choose to complete a., b., or c.

JOURNAL

	DATE		DESCRIPTION	POST. REF.	DEBIT	CREDIT	
1							1
2							2
3							3
4							4
5							5
6							6
7							7
8							8
9							9
10							10
11							11
12							12
13							13
14							14
15							15
16							16
17							17
18							18
19							19
20							20
21							21
22							22
23							23
24							24
25							25
26							26
27							27
28							28
29							29
30							30
31							31
32							32
33							33
34							34
35							35
36							36

APPENDIX 2—PROBLEM 5-15 ___, Concluded

Choose to complete a., b., or c.

JOURNAL

PAGE

	DATE		DESCRIPTION	POST. REF.	DEBIT	CREDIT	
1							1
2							2
3							3
4							4
5							5
6							6
7							7
8							8
9							9
10							10
11							11
12							12
13							13
14							14
15							15
16							16
17							17
18							18
19							19
20							20
21							21
22							22
23							23
24							24
25							25
26							26
27							27
28							28
29							29
30							30
31							31
32							32
33							33
34							34
35							35
36							36

APPENDIX 2—PROBLEM 5-16 ___

Choose to complete a., b., or c.

JOURNAL   PAGE

	DATE		DESCRIPTION	POST. REF.	DEBIT	CREDIT	
1							1
2							2
3							3
4							4
5							5
6							6
7							7
8							8
9							9
10							10
11							11
12							12
13							13
14							14
15							15
16							16
17							17
18							18
19							19
20							20
21							21
22							22
23							23
24							24
25							25
26							26
27							27
28							28
29							29
30							30
31							31
32							32
33							33
34							34
35							35
36							36

APPENDIX 2—PROBLEM 5-16 ___, Concluded

Choose to complete a., b., or c.

JOURNAL

PAGE

	DATE		DESCRIPTION	POST. REF.	DEBIT	CREDIT	
1							1
2							2
3							3
4							4
5							5
6							6
7							7
8							8
9							9
10							10
11							11
12							12
13							13
14							14
15							15
16							16
17							17
18							18
19							19
20							20
21							21
22							22
23							23
24							24
25							25
26							26
27							27
28							28
29							29
30							30
31							31
32							32
33							33
34							34
35							35
36							36

COMPREHENSIVE PROBLEM 2

1., 2., 6., and 9.

ACCOUNT   *Cash*   ACCOUNT NO.   *1010*

DATE		ITEM	POST. REF.	DEBIT	CREDIT	BALANCE	

ACCOUNT   *Accounts Receivable*   ACCOUNT NO.   *1020*

DATE		ITEM	POST. REF.	DEBIT	CREDIT	BALANCE	

ACCOUNT   *Inventory*   ACCOUNT NO.   *1030*

DATE		ITEM	POST. REF.	DEBIT	CREDIT	BALANCE	

COMPREHENSIVE PROBLEM 2, Continued

ACCOUNT   *Store Supplies*   ACCOUNT NO.   *1050*

DATE		ITEM	POST. REF.	DEBIT	CREDIT	BALANCE	

ACCOUNT   *Store Equipment*   ACCOUNT NO.   *1100*

DATE		ITEM	POST. REF.	DEBIT	CREDIT	BALANCE	

ACCOUNT   *Accumulated Depreciation—Store Equipment*   ACCOUNT NO.   *1110*

DATE		ITEM	POST. REF.	DEBIT	CREDIT	BALANCE	

COMPREHENSIVE PROBLEM 2, Continued

ACCOUNT   *Accounts Payable*   ACCOUNT NO.   *2010*

DATE		ITEM	POST. REF.	DEBIT	CREDIT	BALANCE

ACCOUNT   *Salaries Payable*   ACCOUNT NO.   *2020*

DATE		ITEM	POST. REF.	DEBIT	CREDIT	BALANCE

ACCOUNT   *Rocky Hansen, Capital*   ACCOUNT NO.   *3010*

DATE		ITEM	POST. REF.	DEBIT	CREDIT	BALANCE

ACCOUNT   *Rocky Hansen, Withdrawals*   ACCOUNT NO.   *3020*

DATE		ITEM	POST. REF.	DEBIT	CREDIT	BALANCE

COMPREHENSIVE PROBLEM 2, Continued

ACCOUNT   *Income Summary*   ACCOUNT NO.   *3030*

DATE	ITEM	POST. REF.	DEBIT	CREDIT	BALANCE

ACCOUNT   *Sales*   ACCOUNT NO.   *4010*

DATE	ITEM	POST. REF.	DEBIT	CREDIT	BALANCE

ACCOUNT   *Sales Returns and Allowances*   ACCOUNT NO.   *4020*

DATE	ITEM	POST. REF.	DEBIT	CREDIT	BALANCE

COMPREHENSIVE PROBLEM 2, Continued

ACCOUNT   *Sales Discounts*   ACCOUNT NO. *4030*

DATE		ITEM	POST. REF.	DEBIT	CREDIT	BALANCE	

ACCOUNT   *Cost of Goods Sold*   ACCOUNT NO. *5010*

DATE		ITEM	POST. REF.	DEBIT	CREDIT	BALANCE	

ACCOUNT   *Sales Salaries Expense*   ACCOUNT NO. *5110*

DATE		ITEM	POST. REF.	DEBIT	CREDIT	BALANCE	

COMPREHENSIVE PROBLEM 2, Continued

ACCOUNT   *Advertising Expense*   ACCOUNT NO.   *5120*

DATE	ITEM	POST. REF.	DEBIT	CREDIT	BALANCE

ACCOUNT   *Depreciation Expense*   ACCOUNT NO.   *5130*

DATE	ITEM	POST. REF.	DEBIT	CREDIT	BALANCE

ACCOUNT   *Store Supplies Expense*   ACCOUNT NO.   *5140*

DATE	ITEM	POST. REF.	DEBIT	CREDIT	BALANCE

COMPREHENSIVE PROBLEM 2, Continued

ACCOUNT   *Office Salaries Expense*   ACCOUNT NO.   *5210*

DATE		ITEM	POST. REF.	DEBIT	CREDIT	BALANCE	

ACCOUNT   *Rent Expense*   ACCOUNT NO.   *5220*

DATE		ITEM	POST. REF.	DEBIT	CREDIT	BALANCE	

COMPREHENSIVE PROBLEM 2, Continued

1. and 2.

JOURNAL   PAGE 20

	DATE		DESCRIPTION	POST. REF.	DEBIT	CREDIT	
1							1
2							2
3							3
4							4
5							5
6							6
7							7
8							8
9							9
10							10
11							11
12							12
13							13
14							14
15							15
16							16
17							17
18							18
19							19
20							20
21							21
22							22
23							23
24							24
25							25
26							26
27							27
28							28
29							29
30							30
31							31
32							32
33							33
34							34
35							35
36							36

COMPREHENSIVE PROBLEM 2, Continued

JOURNAL

	DATE		DESCRIPTION	POST. REF.	DEBIT	CREDIT	
1							1
2							2
3							3
4							4
5							5
6							6
7							7
8							8
9							9
10							10
11							11
12							12
13							13
14							14
15							15

COMPREHENSIVE PROBLEM 2, Continued

3.

	Unadjusted Trial Balance	

COMPREHENSIVE PROBLEM 2, Continued

4. and 6.

JOURNAL

	DATE		DESCRIPTION	POST. REF.	DEBIT	CREDIT	
1			*Adjusting Entries*				1
2							2
3							3
4							4
5							5
6							6
7							7
8							8
9							9
10							10
11							11
12							12
13							13
14							14
15							15
16							16

COMPREHENSIVE PROBLEM 2, Continued

7.

	Adjusted Trial Balance		

COMPREHENSIVE PROBLEM 2, Continued

8.

Income Statement			

COMPREHENSIVE PROBLEM 2, Continued

Statement of Owner's Equity		

COMPREHENSIVE PROBLEM 2, Continued

	Balance Sheet		

COMPREHENSIVE PROBLEM 2, Continued

9.

JOURNAL

PAGE *23*

	DATE		DESCRIPTION	POST. REF.	DEBIT	CREDIT	
1			*Closing Entries*				1
2							2
3							3
4							4
5							5
6							6
7							7
8							8
9							9
10							10
11							11
12							12
13							13
14							14
15							15
16							16
17							17
18							18
19							19
20							20
21							21
22							22
23							23
24							24
25							25
26							26
27							27
28							28
29							29
30							30
31							31
32							32
33							33
34							34
35							35
36							36

COMPREHENSIVE PROBLEM 2, Continued

10.

Post-Closing Trial Balance		

COMPREHENSIVE PROBLEM 2, Concluded

5. **Optional** *This work sheet is applicable only if the end-of-period spreadsheet (work sheet) is used.*

End-of-Period Spreadsheet (Work Sheet)

	A	B	C	D	E	F	G	H	I	J	K
		Unadjusted Trial Balance		Adjustments		Adjusted Trial Balance		Income Statement		Balance Sheet	
	Account Title	Dr.	Cr.	Dr.	Cr.	Dr.	Cr.	Dr.	Cr.	Dr.	Cr.
6											
7											
8											
9											
10											
11											
12											
13											
14											
15											
16											
17											
18											
19											
20											
21											
22											
23											
24											
25											
26											
27											
28											
29											
30											
31											
32											
33											

EXERCISE 6-1

_____

_____

_____

_____

_____

_____

_____

_____

_____

_____

_____

_____

_____

_____

_____

_____

_____

_____

EXERCISE 6-2

a. _____

_____

_____

_____

_____

b. _____

_____

_____

_____

_____

c. _____

_____

_____

_____

_____

EXERCISE 6-3

a.

Date	Purchases			Cost of Goods Sold			Inventory		
	Quantity	Unit Cost	Total Cost	Quantity	Unit Cost	Total Cost	Quantity	Unit Cost	Total Cost

EXERCISE 6-3 Continued

b.

JOURNAL

PAGE

	DATE		DESCRIPTION	POST. REF.	DEBIT	CREDIT	
1							1
2							2
3							3
4							4
5							5
6							6

EXERCISE 6-3 Continued

c.

Date	Purchases			Cost of goods sold			Inventory		
	Quantity	Unit Cost	Total Cost	Quantity	Unit Cost	Total Cost	Quantity	Total Cost	New Average Unit Cost
Balances									

EXERCISE 6-3 Concluded

d.

JOURNAL

PAGE

	DATE		DESCRIPTION	POST. REF.	DEBIT	CREDIT	
1							1
2							2
3							3
4							4
5							5
6							6

EXERCISE 6-4

a.

Hammocks

Date	Purchases			Cost of Goods Sold			Inventory		
	Quantity	Unit Cost	Total Cost	Quantity	Unit Cost	Total Cost	Quantity	Unit Cost	Total Cost

EXERCISE 6-4 Continued

b.

JOURNAL   PAGE

	DATE		DESCRIPTION	POST. REF.	DEBIT	CREDIT	
1							1
2							2
3							3
4							4
5							5
6							6

EXERCISE 6-4 Continued

c.

Date	Purchases			Cost of goods sold			Inventory		
	Quantity	Unit Cost	Total Cost	Quantity	Unit Cost	Total Cost	Quantity	Total Cost	New Average Unit Cost
Balances									

EXERCISE 6-4 Concluded

d.

JOURNAL

PAGE

	DATE		DESCRIPTION	POST. REF.	DEBIT	CREDIT	
1							1
2							2
3							3
4							4
5							5
6							6

EXERCISE 6-5

a.

Cell Phones

Date	Purchases			Cost of Goods Sold			Inventory		
	Quantity	Unit Cost	Total Cost	Quantity	Unit Cost	Total Cost	Quantity	Unit Cost	Total Cost

EXERCISE 6-5 Concluded

b.

Date	Purchases			Cost of goods sold			Inventory		
	Quantity	Unit Cost	Total Cost	Quantity	Unit Cost	Total Cost	Quantity	Total Cost	New Average Unit Cost
Balances									

EXERCISE 6-6

Watches

Date	Purchases			Cost of Goods Sold			Inventory		
	Quantity	Unit Cost	Total Cost	Quantity	Unit Cost	Total Cost	Quantity	Unit Cost	Total Cost

EXERCISE 6-6 Continued

c.

Date	Purchases			Cost of goods sold			Inventory		
	Quantity	Unit Cost	Total Cost	Quantity	Unit Cost	Total Cost	Quantity	Total Cost	New Average Unit Cost
Balances									

EXERCISE 6-7

_____

_____

EXERCISE 6-8

a. FIFO inventory _____ average cost inventory

b. FIFO cost of goods sold _____ average cost of goods sold

c. FIFO net income _____ average cost net income

d. FIFO income tax _____ average cost income tax

2. _____

_____

_____

_____

_____

_____

_____

_____

_____

_____

_____

_____

_____

EXERCISE 6-9

	A	B	C	D	E	F	G
1			Unit	Unit	Direct		Total	
2		Inventory	Cost	Market	Selling			Lower
3	Item	Quantity	Price	Price	Costs	Cost	NRV	of C and NRV
4	Aquarius	20	$ 80	$ 92	$ 0			
5	Capricorn	50	70	65	250			
6	Leo	8	300	280	0			
7	Scorpio	30	40	30	300			
8	Taurus	100	90	94	0			
9	Total							

EXERCISE 6-10

EXERCISE 6-11

EXERCISE 6-12

EXERCISE 6-13

a.

                                                              Balance Sheet

Inventory.. _____

Current assets .... _____

Total assets .... _____

Owner's equity.. _____

b.

                                                        Income Statement

Cost of goods sold .... _____

Gross profit... _____

Net income .... _____

c.

                                                              Balance Sheet

Inventory.. _____

Current assets .... _____

Total assets .... _____

Owner's equity.. _____

_____

_____

_____

_____

_____

                                                              Income Statement

Cost of goods sold .... _____

Gross profit... _____

Net income .... _____

_____

_____

_____

EXERCISE 6-14

a.   **Balance Sheet**

Inventory.. _____

Current assets... _____

Total assets... _____

Owner's equity .... _____

b.   **Income Statement**

Cost of goods sold .... _____

Gross profit... _____

Net income .... _____

c.   **Balance Sheet**

Inventory.. _____

Current assets... _____

Total assets... _____

Owner's equity .... _____

_____

_____

_____

_____

_____

                                                                      Income Statement

Cost of goods sold .... _____

Gross profit... _____

Net income .... _____

_____

_____

_____

EXERCISE 6-15

_____
_____
_____
_____
_____
_____
_____
_____
_____
_____
_____
_____
_____
_____
_____
_____

APPENDIX 1 EXERCISE 6-16

_____

APPENDIX 1 EXERCISE 6-17

_____

APPENDIX 1 EXERCISE 6-18

_____

APPENDIX 1 EXERCISE 6-19

	A	B	C
1		Cost	Retail
2			
3			
4			
5			
6			
7			
8			

APPENDIX 1 EXERCISE 6-20

a.

	A	B	C
1			Cost
2			
3			
4			
5			
6			
7			
8			

b. _____

_____

_____

_____

_____

APPENDIX 1 EXERCISE 6-21

APPENDIX 1 EXERCISE 6-22

APPENDIX 1 EXERCISE 6-23

a. First-in, first-out method: _____

_____

_____

_____

b. Average cost method: _____

_____

_____

_____

_____

_____

_____

APPENDIX 1 EXERCISE 6-24

a. First-in, first-out method: _____

_____

_____

_____

b. Average cost method: _____

_____

_____

_____

_____

_____

_____

APPENDIX 1 EXERCISE 6-25

	Cost	
Inventory Method	**Inventory**	**Goods Sold**
a. First-in, first-out	_____	_____
b. Average cost	_____	_____

Supporting calculations:

_____

_____

_____

_____

_____

_____

_____

_____

_____

_____

_____

_____

_____

_____

EXERCISE 6-26

a. Apple: _____

American Greetings: _____

b. _____

_____

_____

_____

_____

_____

_____

_____

EXERCISE 6-27

a. Number of Days' Sales in Inventory =

_____

Kroger: _____

_____

Safeway: _____

_____

Inventory Turnover =

_____

Kroger: _____

_____

Safeway: _____

_____

b. _____

_____

_____

_____

_____

_____

_____

_____

_____

_____

_____

PROBLEM 6-1 ___

1.

Date	Purchases			Cost of Goods Sold			Inventory		
	Quantity	Unit Cost	Total Cost	Quantity	Unit Cost	Total Cost	Quantity	Unit Cost	Total Cost

PROBLEM 6-1 ___ , Concluded

2.

JOURNAL   PAGE

	DATE		DESCRIPTION	POST. REF.	DEBIT	CREDIT	
1							1
2							2
3							3
4							4
5							5
6							6
7							7
8							8
9							9
10							10

3. _____

4. _____

5.

JOURNAL   PAGE

	DATE		DESCRIPTION	POST. REF.	DEBIT	CREDIT	
1							1
2							2
3							3
4							4

PROBLEM 6-2 ___

1.

Date	Purchases			Cost of Goods Sold			Inventory		
	Quantity	Unit Cost	Total Cost	Quantity	Unit Cost	Total Cost	Quantity	Unit Cost	Total Cost

PROBLEM 6-2 ___, Concluded

2.

JOURNAL   PAGE

	DATE		DESCRIPTION	POST. REF.	DEBIT	CREDIT	
1							1
2							2
3							3
4							4
5							5
6							6
7							7
8							8
9							9
10							10

3. _____

4. _____

5.

JOURNAL   PAGE

	DATE		DESCRIPTION	POST. REF.	DEBIT	CREDIT	
1							1
2							2
3							3
4							4

PROBLEM 6-3 ___

1.

Date	Purchases			Cost of Goods Sold			Inventory		
	Quantity	Unit Cost	Total Cost	Quantity	Unit Cost	Total Cost	Quantity	Unit Cost	Total Cost

PROBLEM 6-3 ___, Concluded

2.

JOURNAL

PAGE

	DATE		DESCRIPTION	POST. REF.	DEBIT	CREDIT	
1							1
2							2
3							3
4							4
5							5
6							6
7							7
8							8
9							9
10							10

3. _____

4. _____

5.

JOURNAL

PAGE

	DATE		DESCRIPTION	POST. REF.	DEBIT	CREDIT	
1							1
2							2
3							3
4							4

PROBLEM 6-4 ___

1.

Date	Purchases			Cost of Goods Sold			Inventory		
	Quantity	Unit Cost	Total Cost	Quantity	Unit Cost	Total Cost	Quantity	Total Cost	New Average Unit Cost

PROBLEM 6-4 ___ Concluded

2. and 3.

PROBLEM 6-5 ___

1.

Date	Purchases			Cost of Goods Sold			Inventory		
	Quantity	Unit Cost	Total Cost	Quantity	Unit Cost	Total Cost	Quantity	Total Cost	New Average Unit Cost

PROBLEM 6-5 ___ Concluded

2. and 3.

_____

_____

_____

_____

_____

_____

_____

_____

_____

_____

_____

_____

_____

_____

_____

PROBLEM 6-6 ___

1.

Date	Purchases			Cost of Goods Sold			Inventory		
	Quantity	Unit Cost	Total Cost	Quantity	Unit Cost	Total Cost	Quantity	Total Cost	New Average Unit Cost

PROBLEM 6-6 ___, Concluded

2. and 3.

_____

_____

_____

_____

_____

_____

_____

_____

_____

_____

_____

_____

_____

_____

_____

_____

PROBLEM 6-7 ___

1., 2., & 3

	A	B	C	D	E	F	G	H
1								
2				Inventory Sheet December 31, 2010				
3								
4				Unit	Unit	Total		
5		Inventory		Cost	Market			Lower
6	Description	Quantity		Price	Price	Cost	NRV	of C and NRV
7	Alpha 10	38	30	$ 60	$ 57	$1,800	$1,710	
8			8	59		472	456	
9						2,272	2,166	$ 2,166
10	Beta 30	18			180			
11	Charlie 4	30			120			
12								
13								
14	Echo 9	125			26			
15	Frank 6	18			550			
16								
17								
18	George 15	60			15			
19	Killo 6	5			390			
20	Quebec 12	375			6			
21	Romeo 7	90			18			
22								
23								
24	Sierra 3	6			235			
25								
26								
27	Washburn 2	140			20			
28								
29								
30	X-Ray 4	15			745			
31								
32								
33	Total							
34								
35								

This Page Not Used.

PROBLEM 6-8 ___

	A	B	C	D	E	F	G	H
1			Unit	Unit	Direct	Total		
2		Inventory	Cost	Selling	Selling			Lower
3	Model Number	Quantity	Price	Price	Cost	Cost	NRV	of C and NRV
4	236							
5	238							
6	135							
7								
8	333 – a							
9	333 – b							
10	333 – c							
11	Sub-total for 333 series							
12								
13	Total							

a.

_____

b.

_____

_____

_____

c.

_____

_____

_____

This page not used.

APPENDIX 1 PROBLEM 6-9 ___

1.

A	B	C
	Cost	Retail

APPENDIX 1 PROBLEM 6-9 ___ Concluded

2.

a.

	A	B	C
1			
2	a.		Cost
3			
4			
5			
6			
7			
8			
9			
10			
11			
12			
13	b.		
14			
15			
16			
17			

b. _____

APPENDIX 1 PROBLEM 6-10 ___

1.

	A	B	C
1			
2		Cost	Retail
3			
4			
5			
6			
7			
8			
9			
10			
11			
12			

2. _____

_____

_____

_____

APPENDIX 1 PROBLEM 6-10 ___, Concluded

3.

	A	B	C
1			
2			Cost
3			
4			
5			
6			
7			
8			
9			
10			
11			
12			
13			
14			
15			
16			
17			

APPENDIX 2 PROBLEM 6-11 ___

1.   **First-In, First-Out Method**

Model	Quantity	Unit Cost	Total Cost

APPENDIX 2 PROBLEM 6-11 ___ , Concluded

2.   **Average Cost Method**

Model	Quantity	Unit Cost	Total Cost

Computations of unit costs:

_____

_____

_____

_____

_____

_____

_____

3. a. _____

_____

_____

_____

_____

_____

_____

_____

b. _____

_____

_____

_____

APPENDIX 2 PROBLEM 6-12 ___

1.   **First-In, First-Out Method**

Model	Quantity	Unit Cost	Total Cost

APPENDIX 2 PROBLEM 6-12 ___ , Concluded

2.   **Average Cost Method**

Model	Quantity	Unit Cost	Total Cost

EXERCISE 7-1

EXERCISE 7-2

a. _____

_____

_____

_____

b. _____

_____

_____

_____

_____

c. _____

_____

_____

_____

_____

_____

_____

_____

_____

_____

_____

EXERCISE 7-3

1. _____

_____

_____

_____

2. _____

_____

_____

_____

_____

_____

EXERCISE 7-3, Concluded

3. _____

4. _____

EXERCISE 7-4

_____

_____

_____

_____

_____

_____

_____

_____

_____

_____

_____

_____

_____

_____

_____

EXERCISE 7-5

_____

_____

_____

_____

_____

_____

_____

_____

_____

_____

_____

_____

_____

_____

_____

_____

_____

EXERCISE 7-6

EXERCISE 7-7

EXERCISE 7-8

1. _____

2. _____

EXERCISE 7-9

1. _____

   _____

   _____

   _____

   _____

   _____

   _____

2. _____

   _____

   _____

   _____

   _____

   _____

EXERCISE 7-10

1.

a. and b.

JOURNAL   PAGE

	DATE		DESCRIPTION	POST. REF.	DEBIT	CREDIT	
1							1
2							2
3							3
4							4
5							5
6							6
7							7
8							8
9							9
10							10

2.

EXERCISE 7-11

a. and b.

JOURNAL PAGE

	DATE		DESCRIPTION	POST. REF.	DEBIT	CREDIT	
1							1
2							2
3							3
4							4
5							5
6							6
7							7
8							8
9							9
10							10
11							11

EXERCISE 7-12

JOURNAL PAGE

	DATE		DESCRIPTION	POST. REF.	DEBIT	CREDIT	
1							1
2							2
3							3
4							4
5							5
6							6
7							7
8							8
9							9
10							10
11							11
12							12
13							13
14							14
15							15
16							16
17							17
18							18

EXERCISE 7-13

JOURNAL   PAGE

	DATE		DESCRIPTION	POST. REF.	DEBIT	CREDIT	
1							1
2							2
3							3
4							4
5							5
6							6
7							7
8							8
9							9
10							10
11							11
12							12
13							13
14							14

EXERCISE 7-14

a and b

JOURNAL   PAGE

	DATE		DESCRIPTION	POST. REF.	DEBIT	CREDIT	
1							1
2							2
3							3
4							4
5							5
6							6
7							7
8							8
9							9
10							10
11							11
12							12
13							13
14							14

EXERCISE 7-15

1. _____
   _____
   _____
   _____
   _____
   _____
   _____
   _____

2. _____
   _____
   _____
   _____
   _____
   _____
   _____
   _____

EXERCISE 7-16

_____
_____
_____
_____
_____
_____
_____
_____
_____
_____
_____
_____
_____
_____
_____
_____
_____
_____
_____
_____
_____
_____
_____
_____

EXERCISE 7-17

1. _____
_____
_____

2. _____
_____
_____
_____

EXERCISE 7-18

JOURNAL   PAGE

	DATE		DESCRIPTION	POST. REF.	DEBIT	CREDIT	
1							1
2							2
3							3
4							4
5							5
6							6

EXERCISE 7-19

JOURNAL   PAGE

	DATE		DESCRIPTION	POST. REF.	DEBIT	CREDIT	
1							1
2							2
3							3
4							4
5							5
6							6
7							7

EXERCISE 7-20

EXERCISE 7-21

_____
_____
_____
_____
_____
_____
_____
_____
_____
_____
_____
_____
_____
_____
_____
_____
_____
_____
_____
_____
_____
_____
_____
_____
_____

EXERCISE 7-22

a. Addition to the balance per bank: _____

b. Deduction from the balance per bank: _____

c. Addition to the balance per company's records: _____

d. Deduction from the balance per company's records: _____

EXERCISE 7-23

_____

EXERCISE 7-24

Bank Reconciliation

EXERCISE 7-25

JOURNAL

PAGE

	DATE		DESCRIPTION	POST. REF.	DEBIT	CREDIT	
1							1
2							2
3							3
4							4
5							5
6							6
7							7
8							8
9							9

EXERCISE 7-26

JOURNAL   PAGE

	DATE		DESCRIPTION	POST. REF.	DEBIT	CREDIT	
1							1
2							2
3							3
4							4
5							5
6							6
7							7
8							8
9							9

EXERCISE 7-27

JOURNAL   PAGE

	DATE		DESCRIPTION	POST. REF.	DEBIT	CREDIT	
1							1
2							2
3							3
4							4

EXERCISE 7-28

1.

Bank Reconciliation		

2. _____

EXERCISE 7-29

1.

Bank Reconciliation		

2. _____

3. _____

EXERCISE 7-30

JOURNAL   PAGE

	DATE		DESCRIPTION	POST. REF.	DEBIT	CREDIT	
1							1
2							2
3							3
4							4
5							5
6							6

EXERCISE 7-31

_____
_____
_____
_____
_____
_____
_____
_____
_____
_____

`EXERCISE 7-31, Concluded

Bank Reconciliation

EXERCISE 7-32

a. _____

Bank Reconciliation

b.

EXERCISE 7-33

_____

EXERCISE 7-34

a.

_____

b.

_____

EXERCISE 7-35

a.

_____

_____

_____

b.

_____

_____

_____

c.

_____

_____

_____

_____

_____

EXERCISE 7-36

1.

2013: _____

2012: _____

2011: _____

2010: _____

2.

2013: _____

2012: _____

2011: _____

2010: _____

3.

_____

_____

_____

_____

_____

_____

_____

_____

_____

_____

This Page Not Used.

PROBLEM 7-1 ___

_____

_____

_____

_____

_____

_____

_____

_____

_____

_____

_____

_____

_____

_____

_____

_____

_____

_____

_____

_____

_____

_____

_____

_____

_____

_____

_____

_____

_____

_____

_____

_____

_____

_____

_____

_____

_____

_____ *Chapter 7* **505**

_____

This Page Not Used.

PROBLEM 7-2___

_____

_____

_____

_____

_____

_____

_____

_____

_____

_____

_____

_____

_____

_____

_____

_____

_____

This Page Not Used.

PROBLEM 7-3 ___

JOURNAL   PAGE

	DATE		DESCRIPTION	POST. REF.	DEBIT	CREDIT	
1							1
2							2
3							3
4							4
5							5
6							6
7							7
8							8
9							9
10							10
11							11
12							12
13							13
14							14
15							15
16							16
17							17
18							18
19							19
20							20
21							21
22							22
23							23
24							24

This Page Not Used.

PROBLEM 7-4 ___

JOURNAL   PAGE

	DATE		DESCRIPTION	POST. REF.	DEBIT	CREDIT	
1							1
2							2
3							3
4							4
5							5
6							6
7							7
8							8
9							9
10							10
11							11
12							12
13							13
14							14
15							15
16							16

This Page Not Used.

PROBLEM 7-5 ___

JOURNAL   PAGE ____

	DATE		DESCRIPTION	POST. REF.	DEBIT	CREDIT	
1							1
2							2
3							3
4							4
5							5
6							6
7							7
8							8
9							9
10							10
11							11
12							12
13							13
14							14

This Page Not Used.

PROBLEM 7-6 ___

JOURNAL

PAGE _____

	DATE		DESCRIPTION	POST. REF.	DEBIT	CREDIT	
1							1
2							2
3							3
4							4
5							5
6							6
7							7
8							8
9							9
10							10
11							11
12							12
13							13
14							14
15							15

This Page Not Used.

PROBLEM 7-7___

_____
_____
_____
_____
_____
_____
_____
_____
_____
_____
_____
_____
_____
_____
_____
_____
_____
_____
_____
_____
_____
_____
_____
_____
_____
_____
_____
_____
_____
_____
_____
_____
_____
_____
_____
_____
_____
_____
_____
_____
_____
_____
_____
_____
_____

This Page Not Used.

PROBLEM 7-8 ___

1.

Bank Reconciliation		

2.

JOURNAL   PAGE

	DATE	DESCRIPTION	POST. REF.	DEBIT	CREDIT	
1						1
2						2
3						3
4						4
5						5
6						6
7						7

This Page Not Used.

PROBLEM 7-9 ___

1.

Bank Reconciliation		

PROBLEM 7-9 ___, Concluded

2.

JOURNAL   PAGE

	DATE		DESCRIPTION	POST. REF.	DEBIT	CREDIT	
1							1
2							2
3							3
4							4
5							5
6							6
7							7
8							8
9							9
10							10

PROBLEM 7-10 ___

1.

Bank Reconciliation		

PROBLEM 7-10 ___ , Concluded

2.

JOURNAL   PAGE

	DATE		DESCRIPTION	POST. REF.	DEBIT	CREDIT	
1							1
2							2
3							3
4							4
5							5
6							6
7							7
8							8
9							9
10							10

PROBLEM 7-11 ___

1.

Bank Reconciliation		

PROBLEM 7-11 ___, Concluded

2.

JOURNAL

	DATE		DESCRIPTION	POST. REF.	DEBIT	CREDIT	
1							1
2							2
3							3
4							4
5							5
6							6
7							7
8							8
9							9
10							10

PROBLEM 7-12 ___

1.

	Bank Reconciliation		

PROBLEM 7-12 ___, Concluded

2.

JOURNAL   PAGE

	DATE		DESCRIPTION	POST. REF.	DEBIT	CREDIT	
1							1
2							2
3							3
4							4
5							5
6							6
7							7
8							8
9							9
10							10
11							11
12							12
13							13
14							14
15							15
16							16
17							17
18							18
19							19
20							20
21							21
22							22
23							23
24							24

3. _____

4.

_____

_____

_____

_____

_____

_____

PROBLEM 7-13 ___

1.

	Bank Reconciliation		

PROBLEM 7-13 ___, Concluded

2.

_____

_____

_____

_____

_____

3.

JOURNAL   PAGE

	DATE		DESCRIPTION	POST. REF.	DEBIT	CREDIT	
1							1
2							2
3							3
4							4
5							5
6							6
7							7

4. _____

PROBLEM 7-14 ___

1.

	Bank Reconciliation		

PROBLEM 7-14 ___, Concluded

2.

JOURNAL   PAGE

	DATE		DESCRIPTION	POST. REF.	DEBIT	CREDIT	
1							1
2							2
3							3
4							4
5							5
6							6
7							7
8							8
9							9
10							10
11							11
12							12
13							13
14							14
15							15
16							16
17							17
18							18
19							19
20							20
21							21
22							22
23							23
24							24

3. _____

PROBLEM 7-15 ___

1.

Bank Reconciliation		

PROBLEM 7-15 ___ , Concluded

2.

JOURNAL PAGE

	DATE		DESCRIPTION	POST. REF.	DEBIT	CREDIT	
1							1
2							2
3							3
4							4
5							5
6							6
7							7
8							8
9							9
10							10
11							11
12							12
13							13
14							14
15							15
16							16
17							17
18							18
19							19
20							20
21							21
22							22
23							23
24							24

3. _____

EXERCISE 8-1

1. _____   4. _____
2. _____   5. _____
3. _____   6. _____

EXERCISE 8-2

a. _____

_____

_____

b. _____

_____

_____

c. _____

_____

_____

_____

_____

_____

_____

_____

_____

_____

EXERCISE 8-3

JOURNAL

	DATE		DESCRIPTION	POST. REF.	DEBIT	CREDIT	
1							1
2							2
3							3
4							4
5							5
6							6
7							7
8							8
9							9
10							10
11							11
12							12
13							13
14							14
15							15
16							16
17							17
18							18
19							19
20							20

EXERCISE 8-4

JOURNAL   PAGE

	DATE		DESCRIPTION	POST. REF.	DEBIT	CREDIT	
1							1
2							2
3							3
4							4
5							5
6							6
7							7
8							8
9							9
10							10
11							11
12							12
13							13
14							14
15							15
16							16
17							17

EXERCISE 8-5

a.–b.

JOURNAL   PAGE

	DATE		DESCRIPTION	POST. REF.	DEBIT	CREDIT	
1							1
2							2
3							3
4							4
5							5
6							6

EXERCISE 8-6

1.

a. _____   d. _____

b. _____   e. _____

c. _____   f. _____

2.

_____

_____

_____

_____

_____

_____

_____

_____

3.

_____

_____

_____

_____

_____

_____

_____

EXERCISE 8-7

a.

			JOURNAL			PAGE	

	DATE		DESCRIPTION	POST. REF.	DEBIT	CREDIT	
1							1
2							2
3							3
4							4
5							5
6							6
7							7
8							8
9							9
10							10
11							

b.

Balance Sheet (partial)

This page not used.

EXERCISE 8-8

BALANCE	NOT PAST DUE	DAYS PAST DUE			
		1–30	31–60	61–90	OVER 90

EXERCISE 8-9

JOURNAL   PAGE _____

DATE	DESCRIPTION	POST. REF.	DEBIT	CREDIT
1				
2				
3				
4				
5				

EXERCISE 8-10

Age Interval	Balance	Estimated Uncollectible Accounts	
		Percent	Amount
Not past due	$567,000	½%	$ _____
1–30 days past due	58,000	3	_____
31–60 days past due	29,000	7	_____
61–90 days past due	20,500	15	_____
Over 91 days past due	25,500	60	_____
Total	$700,000		$ _____

EXERCISE 8-11

a.   **JOURNAL**   PAGE

	DATE	DESCRIPTION	POST. REF.	DEBIT	CREDIT	
1						1
2						2
3						3
4						4
5						5

b.__

_____

_____

EXERCISE 8-12

JOURNAL

	DATE		DESCRIPTION	POST. REF.	DEBIT	CREDIT	
1							1
2							2
3							3
4							4
5							5
6							6
7							7
8							8
9							9
10							10
11							11
12							12
13							13
14							14
15							15
16							16
17							17
18							18
19							19
20							20
21							21
22							22
23							23
24							24
25							25
26							26
27							27
28							28
29							29
30							30
31							31
32							32
33							33
34							34
35							35

EXERCISE 8-13

a.

		JOURNAL					PAGE	

	DATE		DESCRIPTION	POST. REF.	DEBIT	CREDIT	
1							1
2							2
3							3
4							4
5							5
6							6
7							7
8							8
9							9
10							10
11							11
12							12
13							13
14							14
15							15
16							16
17							17
18							18
19							19
20							20
21							21
22							22
23							23
24							24
25							25
26							26

Computations:

_____

_____

_____

_____

_____

_____

_____

_____

EXERCISE 8-13, Concluded

b. _____

EXERCISE 8-14

JOURNAL   PAGE

	DATE		DESCRIPTION	POST. REF.	DEBIT	CREDIT	
1							1
2							2
3							3
4							4
5							5
6							6
7							7
8							8
9							9
10							10
11							11
12							12
13							13
14							14
15							15
16							16

EXERCISE 8-15

JOURNAL   PAGE

	DATE		DESCRIPTION	POST. REF.	DEBIT	CREDIT	
1							1
2							2
3							3
4							4
5							5
6							6

EXERCISE 8-16

a.

JOURNAL   PAGE

	DATE		DESCRIPTION	POST. REF.	DEBIT	CREDIT	
1							1
2							2
3							3
4							4
5							5
6							6

b. _____

EXERCISE 8-17

a.

JOURNAL   PAGE

	DATE		DESCRIPTION	POST. REF.	DEBIT	CREDIT	
1							1
2							2
3							3
4							4
5							5
6							6

b. _____

EXERCISE 8-18

JOURNAL   PAGE

	DATE		DESCRIPTION	POST. REF.	DEBIT	CREDIT	
1							1
2							2
3							3
4							4

EXERCISE 8-19

1. _____

2. _____

3. _____

4. _____

5. _____

6. _____

7. _____

EXERCISE 8-20

1.

JOURNAL   PAGE

	DATE		DESCRIPTION	POST. REF.	DEBIT	CREDIT	
1							1
2							2
3							3
4							4
5							5
6							6
7							7
8							8
9							9
10							10
11							11
12							12
13							13
14							14
15							15
16							16
17							17
18							18

2.

_____

_____

EXERCISE 8-21

JOURNAL   PAGE

	DATE		DESCRIPTION	POST. REF.	DEBIT	CREDIT	
1							1
2							2
3							3
4							4
5							5
6							6
7							7
8							8
9							9
10							10
11							11

EXERCISE 8-22

JOURNAL   PAGE ____

	DATE		DESCRIPTION	POST. REF.	DEBIT	CREDIT	
1							1
2							2
3							3
4							4
5							5
6							6
7							7
8							8
9							9
10							10
11							11
12							12
13							13
14							14
15							15
16							16
17							17
18							18
19							19
20							20
21							21
22							22
23							23
24							24
25							25
26							26
27							27
28							28
29							29
30							30
31							31
32							32
33							33
34							34
35							35
36							36

EXERCISE 8-23

a.

_____

_____

_____

_____

_____

_____

b.

_____

Balance Sheet			

APPENDIX EXERCISE 8-24

a and b.

_____

_____

_____

_____

_____

c.

_____

_____

_____

d.

_____

_____

EXERCISE 8-25

a. and b.

	2010	**2009**
Accounts receivable turnover	_____	_____
Days' sales in receivables	_____	_____

c. _____

_____

_____

_____

_____

d. _____

_____

_____

EXERCISE 8-26

a. 2011: _____

2010: _____

b. 2011: _____

2010: _____

c. _____

_____

_____

_____

_____

_____

_____

_____

EXERCISE 8-27

a. and b.

	For the Period Ending	
	Jan. 31, 2011	**Jan 31, 2010**
Accounts receivable turnover	_____	_____
Days' sales in receivables	_____	_____

c. _____

_____

_____

_____

_____

_____

_____

_____

This page not used.

PROBLEM 8-1 ___

1.

Allowance for Doubtful Accounts

PROBLEM 8-1 ___, Concluded

2.

JOURNAL

PAGE

	DATE		DESCRIPTION	POST. REF.	DEBIT	CREDIT	
1							1
2							2
3							3
4							4
5							5
6							6
7							7
8							8
9							9
10							10
11							11
12							12
13							13
14							14
15							15
16							16
17							17
18							18
19							19
20							20
21							21
22							22
23							23
24							24
25							25
26							26
27							27
28							28
29							29
30							30
31							31
32							32
33							33

3. _____

PROBLEM 8-2 ___

1.

Allowance for Doubtful Accounts

PROBLEM 8-2 ___, Concluded

2.

JOURNAL   PAGE

	DATE		DESCRIPTION	POST. REF.	DEBIT	CREDIT	
1							1
2							2
3							3
4							4
5							5
6							6
7							7
8							8
9							9
10							10
11							11
12							12
13							13
14							14
15							15
16							16
17							17
18							18
19							19
20							20
21							21
22							22
23							23
24							24
25							25
26							26
27							27
28							28
29							29
30							30
31							31
32							32
33							33

3. _____

PROBLEM 8-3 ___

1.

	A	B	C	D	E	F	G
1							
2							
3					Days Past Due		
4	Customer	Balance	Not Past Due	1–30	31–60	61–90	Over 90
5							
6							
30							
31							
32							
33							
34							
35							
36							
37							
38							
39							
40							
41							
42							

2.

JOURNAL   PAGE ____

	DATE	DESCRIPTION	POST. REF.	DEBIT	CREDIT	
1						1
2						2
3						3
4						4
5						5
6						6
7						7

3. _____

This Page Not Used.

PROBLEM 8-4 ___

1. and 2.

JOURNAL

	DATE		DESCRIPTION	POST. REF.	DEBIT	CREDIT	
1							1
2							2
3							3
4							4
5							5
6							6
7							7
8							8
9							9
10							10
11							11
12							12
13							13
14							14
15							15
16							16
17							17
18							18
19							19
20							20
21							21
22							22
23							23
24							24

This Page Not Used.

PROBLEM 8-5 ___

	DATE		DESCRIPTION	POST. REF.	DEBIT	CREDIT	
1							1
2							2
3							3
4							4
5							5
6							6
7							7
8							8
9							9
10							10
11							11
12							12
13							13
14							14
15							15
16							16
17							17
18							18
19							19
20							20
21							21
22							22
23							23
24							24
25							25
26							26
27							27
28							28
29							29
30							30
31							31
32							32
33							33
34							34

JOURNAL   PAGE

This Page Not Used.

PROBLEM 8-6 ___

1.

Note	(a) Due Date	(b) Interest Due at Maturity
1.		
2.		
3.		
4.		

2., 3., and 4.

JOURNAL

PAGE

	DATE		DESCRIPTION	POST. REF.	DEBIT	CREDIT	
1							1
2							2
3							3
4							4
5							5
6							6
7							7
8							8
9							9
10							10
11							11
12							12
13							13
14							14
15							15
16							16
17							17
18							18
19							19
20							20
21							21
22							22
23							23
24							24

This page not used.

PROBLEM 8-7 ___

	JOURNAL			PAGE	

	DATE		DESCRIPTION	POST. REF.	DEBIT	CREDIT	
1							1
2							2
3							3
4							4
5							5
6							6
7							7
8							8
9							9
10							10
11							11
12							12
13							13
14							14
15							15
16							16
17							17
18							18
19							19
20							20
21							21
22							22
23							23
24							24
25							25
26							26
27							27
28							28
29							29
30							30
31							31
32							32
33							33
34							34

This page not used.

PROBLEM 8-8 ___

	DATE		DESCRIPTION	POST. REF.	DEBIT	CREDIT	
1							1
2							2
3							3
4							4
5							5
6							6
7							7
8							8
9							9
10							10
11							11
12							12
13							13
14							14
15							15
16							16
17							17
18							18
19							19
20							20
21							21
22							22
23							23
24							24
25							25
26							26
27							27
28							28
29							29
30							30
31							31
32							32
33							33
34							34

This page not used.

PROBLEM 8-9 ___

JOURNAL   PAGE

	DATE		DESCRIPTION	POST. REF.	DEBIT	CREDIT	
1							1
2							2
3							3
4							4
5							5
6							6
7							7
8							8
9							9
10							10
11							11
12							12
13							13
14							14
15							15
16							16
17							17
18							18
19							19
20							20
21							21
22							22
23							23
24							24
25							25
26							26
27							27
28							28
29							29
30							30
31							31
32							32
33							33
34							34

This page not used.

PROBLEM 8-10 ___

JOURNAL

	DATE		DESCRIPTION	POST. REF.	DEBIT	CREDIT	
1							1
2							2
3							3
4							4
5							5
6							6
7							7
8							8
9							9
10							10
11							11
12							12
13							13
14							14
15							15
16							16
17							17
18							18
19							19
20							20
21							21
22							22
23							23
24							24
25							25
26							26
27							27
28							28
29							29
30							30
31							31
32							32
33							33
34							34

PROBLEM 8-10 ___, Concluded

2.

		Balance Sheet		

3.

JOURNAL   PAGE

	DATE		DESCRIPTION	POST. REF.	DEBIT	CREDIT	
1							1
2							2
3							3
4							4
5							5

EXERCISE 9-1

a. New printing press costs debited to the asset account:

_____
_____
_____
_____

EXERCISE 9-2

_____
_____
_____
_____

EXERCISE 9-3

a. _____
_____
_____

b. _____
_____
_____

EXERCISE 9-4

EXERCISE 9-5

_____

_____

_____

_____

EXERCISE 9-6

_____

_____

_____

_____

EXERCISE 9-7

1. _____
2. _____
3. _____
4. _____
5. _____
6. _____
7. _____

EXERCISE 9-8

1. _____
2. _____
3. _____
4. _____
5. _____
6. _____
7. _____

EXERCISE 9-9

JOURNAL   PAGE

	DATE		DESCRIPTION	POST. REF.	DEBIT	CREDIT	
1							1
2							2
3							3
4							4
5							5
6							6
7							7
8							8
9							9

EXERCISE 9-10

a. _____

_____

_____

_____

b. _____

_____

_____

_____

EXERCISE 9-11

a. 4 years: _____

b. 8 years: _____

c. 10 years: _____

d. 25 years: _____

e. 40 years: _____

f. 50 years: _____

EXERCISE 9-12

_____

_____

EXERCISE 9-13

_____

_____

_____

_____

EXERCISE 9-14

a.

Truck No.	Rate per km	kms Operated	Credit to Accumulated Amortization
1	_____	_____	$_____
2	_____	_____	$_____
3	_____	_____	$_____
4	_____	_____	$_____
Total			$_____

b.

JOURNAL　　　　　　　　　　　　　　　PAGE

	DATE		DESCRIPTION	POST. REF.	DEBIT	CREDIT	
1							1
2							2
3							3
4							4

EXERCISE 9-15

a. Straight-line method:

First year: _____

Second year: _____

b. Double-declining-balance method:

First year: _____

Second year: _____

EXERCISE 9-16

a. Straight-line method:

_____

b. Double-declining-balance method:

Year 1: _____

Year 2: _____

	Year 1	Year 2

EXERCISE 9-17

a. Straight-line method:

Year 1: _____

Year 2: _____

b. Double-declining-balance method:

Year 1: _____

Year 2: _____

_____

_____

_____

_____

_____

EXERCISE 9-18

a. _____

b. _____

c. _____

_____

EXERCISE 9-18, Concluded

	2014	2013	

EXERCISE 9-19

a. _____

b. _____

c. _____

EXERCISE 9-20

a. _____

b. _____

c. _____

d. _____

EXERCISE 9-21

a.

EXERCISE 9-21, Concluded

b.(1) and (2)

JOURNAL   PAGE

	DATE		DESCRIPTION	POST. REF.	DEBIT	CREDIT	
1							1
2							2
3							3
4							4
5							5
6							6
7							7
8							8
9							9
10							10

EXERCISE 9-22

a. 2012: _____

2013: _____

2014: _____

b. _____

EXERCISE 9-22, Concluded

c. and d.

JOURNAL   PAGE

	DATE		DESCRIPTION	POST. REF.	DEBIT	CREDIT	
1							1
2							2
3							3
4							4
5							5
6							6
7							7
8							8
9							9
10							10
11							11
12							12
13							13
14							14
15							15
16							16
17							17

EXERCISE 9-23

a. _____

_____

b.

JOURNAL   PAGE

	DATE		DESCRIPTION	POST. REF.	DEBIT	CREDIT	
1							1
2							2
3							3
4							4

EXERCISE 9-24

a. _____

_____

b.

JOURNAL   PAGE

	DATE		DESCRIPTION	POST. REF.	DEBIT	CREDIT	
1							1
2							2
3							3
4							4

EXERCISE 9-25

a.

	Current Year	Preceding Year	

_____

_____

_____

_____

_____

_____

EXERCISE 9-25, Concluded

b.

_____

_____

_____

_____

_____

_____

_____

_____

_____

c.

_____

_____

_____

_____

_____

EXERCISE 9-26

_____

_____

_____

_____

_____

_____

_____

_____

_____

_____

_____

_____

_____

_____

_____

EXERCISE 9-27

a. _____

b. _____

_____

EXERCISE 9-28

a. _____

b. _____

_____

_____

_____

_____

_____

_____

This page not used.

PROBLEM 9-1 ___

1.

Item	Land	Land Improvements	Building	Other Accounts
a.				
b.				
c.				
d.				
e.				
f.				
g.				
h.				
i.				
j.				
k.				
l.				
m.				
n.				
o.				
p.				
q.				
r.				

2.

Total				

*Indicates receipt

3.

_____

_____

_____

PROBLEM 9-1 ___, Concluded

4.

_____

_____

_____

_____

_____

_____

PROBLEM 9-2 ___

1.

	Depreciation Expense		
Year	a. Straight-Line Method	b. Units-of-Production Method	c. Double-Declining-Balance Method
_____	_____	_____	_____
_____	_____	_____	_____
_____	_____	_____	_____
_____	_____	_____	_____
Total	_____	_____	_____

2. and 3

Calculations:

_____

_____

_____

_____

_____

_____

_____

_____

_____

_____

_____

_____

_____

_____

_____

_____

_____

_____

_____

_____

_____

_____

_____

_____

_____

_____

This Page Not Used.

PROBLEM 9-3 ___

a.

Straight-Line Method

Year	Calculations	Depreciation Expense
2013		
2014		
2015		
2016		

b.

Units-of-Production Method

Year	Calculations	Depreciation Expense
2013		
2014		
2015		
2016		

c.

Double-Declining-Balance Method

Year	Calculations	Depreciation Expense
2013		
2014		
2015		
2016		

This Page Not Used.

PROBLEM 9-4 ___

1. a.

Straight-Line Method

Year	Depreciation Expense	Accumulated Depreciation, End of Year	Carrying Amount, End of Year
1			
2			
3			
4			

b.

Double-Declining-Balance Method

Year	Depreciation Expense	Accumulated Depreciation, End of Year	Carrying Amount, End of Year
1			
2			
3			
4			

PROBLEM 9-4 ___, Concluded

2.

JOURNAL   PAGE

	DATE		DESCRIPTION	POST. REF.	DEBIT	CREDIT	
1							1
2							2
3							3
4							4
5							5
6							6

3.

JOURNAL   PAGE

	DATE		DESCRIPTION	POST. REF.	DEBIT	CREDIT	
1							1
2							2
3							3
4							4
5							5
6							6

PROBLEM 9-5 ___

JOURNAL

	DATE		DESCRIPTION	POST. REF.	DEBIT	CREDIT	
1							1
2							2
3							3
4							4
5							5
6							6
7							7
8							8
9							9
10							10
11							11
12							12
13							13
14							14
15							15
16							16
17							17
18							18
19							19
20							20
21							21
22							22
23							23
24							24
25							25
26							26
27							27
28							28
29							29
30							30
31							31
32							32
33							33
34							34
35							35
36							36

PROBLEM 9-5 ___, Concluded

JOURNAL   PAGE

	DATE		DESCRIPTION	POST. REF.	DEBIT	CREDIT	
1							1
2							2
3							3
4							4
5							5
6							6
7							7
8							8
9							9
10							10
11							11
12							12
13							13
14							14
15							15
16							16
17							17
18							18
19							19
20							20
21							21
22							22
23							23
24							24
25							25
26							26
27							27
28							28
29							29
30							30
31							31
32							32
33							33
34							34
35							35
36							36

PROBLEM 9-6 ___

JOURNAL

	DATE		DESCRIPTION	POST. REF.	DEBIT	CREDIT	
1							1
2							2
3							3
4							4
5							5
6							6
7							7
8							8
9							9
10							10
11							11
12							12
13							13
14							14
15							15
16							16
17							17
18							18
19							19
20							20
21							21
22							22
23							23
24							24
25							25
26							26
27							27
28							28
29							29
30							30
31							31
32							32
33							33
34							34
35							35
36							36

PROBLEM 9-6 ___ , Concluded

JOURNAL

	DATE		DESCRIPTION	POST. REF.	DEBIT	CREDIT	
1							1
2							2
3							3
4							4
5							5
6							6
7							7
8							8
9							9
10							10
11							11
12							12
13							13
14							14
15							15
16							16
17							17
18							18
19							19
20							20
21							21
22							22
23							23
24							24
25							25
26							26
27							27
28							28
29							29
30							30
31							31
32							32
33							33
34							34
35							35
36							36

PROBLEM 9-7 ___

1.

a. _____
   _____

b. _____
   _____

c. _____
   _____
   _____

2.

JOURNAL   PAGE

	DATE		DESCRIPTION	POST. REF.	DEBIT	CREDIT	
1							1
2							2
3							3
4							4
5							5
6							6
7							7
8							8
9							9
10							10
11							11
12							12

Notes

EXERCISE 10-1

EXERCISE 10-2

JOURNAL   PAGE

	DATE		DESCRIPTION	POST. REF.	DEBIT	CREDIT	
1							1
2							2
3							3
4							4
5							5
6							6
7							7
8							8
9							9
10							10
11							11
12							12
13							13
14							14
15							15

EXERCISE 10-3

Choice of a., b., or c.

JOURNAL   PAGE

	DATE		DESCRIPTION	POST. REF.	DEBIT	CREDIT	
1							1
2							2
3							3
4							4
5							5
6							6
7							7
8							8
9							9
10							10
11							11
12							12
13							13
14							14
15							15
16							16
17							17
18							18

EXERCISE 10-4

JOURNAL   PAGE

	DATE		DESCRIPTION	POST. REF.	DEBIT	CREDIT	
1							1
2							2
3							3
4							4
5							5
6							6
7							7
8							8
9							9
10							10
11							11
12							12
13							13
14							14
15							15
16							16
17							17
18							18

EXERCISE 10-5

JOURNAL

	DATE		DESCRIPTION	POST. REF.	DEBIT	CREDIT	
1							1
2							2
3							3
4							4
5							5
6							6
7							7
8							8
9							9
10							10
11							11
12							12
13							13
14							14
15							15
16							16
17							17
18							18

EXERCISE 10-6

JOURNAL

	DATE		DESCRIPTION	POST. REF.	DEBIT	CREDIT	
1							1
2							2
3							3
4							4
5							5
6							6
7							7
8							8
9							9
10							10
11							11
12							12
13							13
14							14
15							15
16							16
17							17
18							18
19							19
20							20

EXERCISE 10-7

a. (1)_____

   (2)_____

b. (1) _____

   (2) _____

c. _____

_____

_____

_____

_____

_____

_____

_____

_____

_____

_____

_____

EXERCISE 10-8

a. and b.

JOURNAL

PAGE

	DATE		DESCRIPTION	POST. REF.	DEBIT	CREDIT	
1							1
2							2
3							3
4							4
5							5
6							6
7							7
8							8
9							9
10							10
11							11
12							12
13							13
14							14

EXERCISE 10-9

a. and b.

JOURNAL   PAGE

	DATE		DESCRIPTION	POST. REF.	DEBIT	CREDIT	
1							1
2							2
3							3
4							4
5							5
6							6
7							7
8							8
9							9

EXERCISE 10-10

a.–c.

JOURNAL   PAGE

	DATE		DESCRIPTION	POST. REF.	DEBIT	CREDIT	
1							1
2							2
3							3
4							4
5							5
6							6
7							7
8							8
9							9
10							10
11							11
12							12

EXERCISE 10-11

EXERCISE 10-12

a. _____

_____

b. _____

_____

c. _____

_____

d. _____

_____

EXERCISE 10-13

a. and b.

JOURNAL   PAGE

	DATE		DESCRIPTION	POST. REF.	DEBIT	CREDIT	
1							1
2							2
3							3
4							4
5							5
6							6
7							7
8							8

EXERCISE 10-14

a. _____

_____

_____

_____

_____

_____

_____

b.

JOURNAL   PAGE

	DATE		DESCRIPTION	POST. REF.	DEBIT	CREDIT	
1							1
2							2
3							3
4							4
5							5

EXERCISE 10-15

a. and b.

JOURNAL   PAGE

	DATE		DESCRIPTION	POST. REF.	DEBIT	CREDIT	
1							1
2							2
3							3
4							4
5							5
6							6
7							7
8							8

EXERCISE 10-16

a., b., c., d.

	JOURNAL				PAGE

	DATE		DESCRIPTION	POST. REF.	DEBIT	CREDIT	
1							1
2							2
3							3
4							4
5							5
6							6
7							7
8							8
9							9
10							10
11							11
12							12
13							13
14							14
15							15
16							16

e.

_____

_____

_____

EXERCISE 10-17

a.

		JOURNAL			PAGE

	DATE		DESCRIPTION	POST. REF.	DEBIT	CREDIT	
1							1
2							2
3							3
4							4
5							5
6							6

b.

_____

_____

_____

EXERCISE 10-18

_____
_____
_____
_____
_____
_____
_____
_____
_____
_____
_____
_____
_____
_____
_____
_____
_____
_____
_____

EXERCISE 10-19

a.

JOURNAL PAGE

	DATE		DESCRIPTION	POST. REF.	DEBIT	CREDIT	
1							1
2							2
3							3
4							4
5							5
6							6
7							7
8							8

EXERCISE 10-19 Concluded

b.

_____

_____

_____

_____

_____

_____

_____

_____

_____

_____

_____

EXERCISE 10-20

1. _____

_____

_____

_____

_____

2. _____

_____

_____

_____

_____

3._____

_____

_____

_____

_____

EXERCISE 10-21

a.

JOURNAL   PAGE

	DATE		DESCRIPTION	POST. REF.	DEBIT	CREDIT	
1							1
2							2
3							3
4							4
5							5
6							6
7							7
8							8

b.

_____

_____

_____

_____

_____

_____

_____

_____

_____

_____

_____

EXERCISE 10-22

a.

	DATE		DESCRIPTION	POST. REF.	DEBIT	CREDIT	
1							1
2							2
3							3
4							4
5							5
6							6
7							7
8							8

JOURNAL   PAGE

b.

_____

_____

_____

_____

_____

_____

_____

_____

_____

_____

_____

EXERCISE 10-23

a.

b.

c.

JOURNAL

PAGE

	DATE		DESCRIPTION	POST. REF.	DEBIT	CREDIT	
1							1
2							2
3							3
4							4
5							5
6							6
7							7
8							8
9							9
10							10
11							11
12							12
13							13
14							14
15							15
16							16
17							17
18							18

EXERCISE 10-24

	Consultant	Computer Programmer	Administrator
Regular earnings	$ _____	$ _____	$ _____
Overtime earnings	_____	_____	_____
Gross pay	$ _____	$ _____	$ _____
Less: CPP..	$ _____	$ _____	$ _____
EI...	_____	_____	_____
Provincial Income taxes withheld	_____	_____	_____
Federal income taxes	_____	_____	_____
	$ _____	$ _____	$ _____
Net pay	$ _____	$ _____	$ _____

Calculations:

_____

_____

_____

_____

_____

_____

_____

_____

_____

EXERCISE 10-25

a.

b. and c.

JOURNAL

PAGE

	DATE		DESCRIPTION	POST. REF.	DEBIT	CREDIT	
1							1
2							2
3							3
4							4
5							5
6							6
7							7
8							8
9							9
10							10
11							11
12							12

EXERCISE 10-25, Concluded

d.

_____

_____

_____

_____

_____

EXERCISE 10-26

a.

b.

JOURNAL   PAGE

	DATE		DESCRIPTION	POST. REF.	DEBIT	CREDIT	
1							1
2							2
3							3
4							4
5							5
6							6
7							7
8							8
9							9
10							10
11							11
12							12
13							13
14							14
15							15
16							16
17							17
18							18
19							19

EXERCISE 10-27

a.

JOURNAL

PAGE

	DATE	DESCRIPTION	POST. REF.	DEBIT	CREDIT	
1						1
2						2
3						3
4						4
5						5
6						6
7						7
8						8
9						9
10						10
11						11

b.

JOURNAL

PAGE

	DATE	DESCRIPTION	POST. REF.	DEBIT	CREDIT	
1						1
2						2
3						3
4						4
5						5
6						6
7						7
8						8

EXERCISE 10-28

a.

	DATE		DESCRIPTION	POST. REF.	DEBIT	CREDIT	
1							1
2							2
3							3
4							4
5							5
6							6
7							7
8							8
9							9

JOURNAL   PAGE

b.

JOURNAL   PAGE

	DATE		DESCRIPTION	POST. REF.	DEBIT	CREDIT	
1							1
2							2
3							3
4							4
5							5
6							6
7							7
8							8
9							9

EXERCISE 10-29

_____

_____

_____

_____

_____

_____

_____

_____

EXERCISE 10-30

a. _____

_____

_____

_____

_____

b. _____

_____

_____

_____

_____

c. _____

_____

_____

_____

_____

d. _____

_____

_____

_____

_____

e. _____

_____

_____

_____

_____

EXERCISE 10-31

_____

_____

_____

_____

_____

_____

_____

_____

_____

_____

_____

_____

_____

_____

EXERCISE 10-32

JOURNAL   PAGE

	DATE		DESCRIPTION	POST. REF.	DEBIT	CREDIT	
1							1
2							2
3							3

EXERCISE 10-33

JOURNAL   PAGE

	DATE		DESCRIPTION	POST. REF.	DEBIT	CREDIT	
1							1
2							2
3							3

EXERCISE 10-34

a. December 31, 2014: _____

_____

December 31, 2015: _____

_____

b. _____

_____

_____

_____

_____

_____

_____

_____

_____

_____

_____

_____

_____

_____

_____

_____

EXERCISE 10-35

a.

	Company 1:	Company 2:
Quick Ratio:	_____	_____
Computations:		

_____

_____

_____

_____

_____

_____

_____

_____

_____

_____

_____

b. _____

_____

_____

_____

_____

_____

_____

_____

_____

_____

_____

_____

_____

_____

_____

_____

PROBLEM 10-1 ___
Choice of a., b., c., or d.

JOURNAL

PAGE ____

	DATE		DESCRIPTION	POST. REF.	DEBIT	CREDIT	
1							1
2							2
3							3
4							4
5							5
6							6
7							7
8							8
9							9
10							10
11							11
12							12
13							13
14							14
15							15
16							16
17							17
18							18
19							19
20							20
21							21
22							22
23							23
24							24
25							25
26							26
27							27
28							28
29							29
30							30
31							31
32							32
33							33
34							34
35							35
36							36

This page not used.

PROBLEM 10-2 ___

1. Choice of a., b., c., or d.

JOURNAL   PAGE

	DATE		DESCRIPTION	POST. REF.	DEBIT	CREDIT	
1							1
2							2
3							3
4							4
5							5
6							6
7							7
8							8
9							9
10							10
11							11
12							12
13							13
14							14
15							15
16							16
17							17
18							18
19							19
20							20
21							21
22							22
23							23
24							24
25							25
26							26
27							27
28							28
29							29
30							30
31							31
32							32
33							33
34							34
35							35
36							36

PROBLEM 10-2 ___ , Concluded

2. Choice of a., b., c., or d.

JOURNAL

PAGE

	DATE		DESCRIPTION	POST. REF.	DEBIT	CREDIT	
1							1
2							2
3							3
4							4
5							5
6							6

PROBLEM 10-3 ___

1. Choice of a, b, c, or d

JOURNAL

	DATE		DESCRIPTION	POST. REF.	DEBIT	CREDIT	
1							1
2							2
3							3
4							4
5							5
6							6
7							7
8							8
9							9
10							10
11							11
12							12
13							13
14							14
15							15
16							16
17							17
18							18
19							19
20							20
21							21
22							22
23							23
24							24
25							25
26							26
27							27
28							28
29							29
30							30
31							31
32							32
33							33
34							34
35							35
36							36

PROBLEM 10-3 ___ , Concluded

2. Choice of a, b, c, or d

JOURNAL

	DATE		DESCRIPTION	POST. REF.	DEBIT	CREDIT	
1							1
2							2
3							3
4							4
5							5
6							6

PROBLEM 10-4 ___

1. through 4.

JOURNAL   PAGE

	DATE		DESCRIPTION	POST. REF.	DEBIT	CREDIT	
1							1
2							2
3							3
4							4
5							5
6							6
7							7
8							8
9							9
10							10
11							11
12							12
13							13
14							14
15							15
16							16
17							17
18							18
19							19
20							20
21							21
22							22
23							23
24							24
25							25
26							26
27							27
28							28
29							29
30							30
31							31
32							32
33							33
34							34
35							35
36							36

PROBLEM 10-4 ___, Concluded

5. through 7.

JOURNAL

	DATE		DESCRIPTION	POST. REF.	DEBIT	CREDIT	
1							1
2							2
3							3
4							4
5							5
6							6
7							7
8							8
9							9
10							10
11							11
12							12
13							13
14							14
15							15
16							16
17							17
18							18
19							19
20							20
21							21
22							22
23							23
24							24
25							25
26							26
27							27
28							28
29							29
30							30
31							31
32							32
33							33
34							34
35							35
36							36

PROBLEM 10-5 ___

1.

		Deductions					Paid
	Gross	CPP	EI	Prov. Taxes	Fed. Taxes	Total	Net Pay
J. Carson							
R. Docker							

2.

JOURNAL   PAGE

	DATE		DESCRIPTION	POST. REF.	DEBIT	CREDIT	
1							1
2							2
3							3
4							4
5							5
6							6
7							7
8							8
9							9
10							10
11							11
12							12
13							13
14							14

This page not used.

PROBLEM 10-6A

PAYROLL FOR THE WEEK ENDED April 10, 2015

Name	Rate	Hours	EARNINGS Reg	OT	Gross	DEDUCTIONS CPP	EI	Prov. Income Taxes	Fed. Income Taxes	RRSP	United Way	Total	Paid Net pay	Chq No.	Accounts Debited Sales Salaries Expense	Office Salaries Expense	Delivery Salaries Expense
R. Baron	25.00	40.00	1,000.00	-	1,000.00	46.17	18.30	59.70	118.85	50.00	15.00	308.02	691.98	801			1,000.00
J. Chasson	32.00	44.00	1,408.00	64.00	1,472.00	69.53	26.94	108.50	223.15	73.60	10.00	511.72	960.28	802	1,472.00		
M. Davis	27.00	41.00	1,107.00	13.50	1,120.50	52.13	20.51	71.60	146.55	56.03	15.00	361.81	758.69	803		1,120.50	
R. Franks	29.00	40.00	1,160.00	-	1,160.00	54.09	21.23	74.90	154.50	58.00	25.00	387.72	772.28	804		1,160.00	
S. Ingrams	32.00	43.00	1,376.00	48.00	1,424.00	67.16	26.06	103.25	212.55	71.20	5.00	485.22	938.78	805			1,424.00
L. Lewis	26.00	40.00	1,040.00	-	1,040.00	48.15	19.03	72.70	128.10	52.00	10.00	329.98	710.02	806		1,040.00	
L. Toner	30.00	46.00	1,380.00	90.00	1,470.00	69.43	26.90	108.50	223.15	73.50	25.00	526.48	943.52	807	1,470.00		
F. Ventresca	45.00	40.00	1,800.00	-	1,800.00	85.77	32.94	159.50	303.15	90.00	-	671.36	1,128.64	808	1,800.00		
K. Wong	25.00	40.00	1,000.00	-	1,000.00	46.17	18.30	59.70	118.85	50.00	15.00	308.02	691.98	809			1,000.00
			11,271.00	215.50	11,486.50	538.60	210.20	818.35	1,628.85	574.33	120.00	3,890.32	7,596.18		4,742.00	3,320.50	3,424.00

PROBLEM 10-6B

PAYROLL FOR THE WEEK ENDED July 3, 2015

Name	Rate	Hours	EARNINGS			DEDUCTIONS							Paid		Accounts Debited		
			Reg	OT	Gross	CPP	EI	Prov. Income Taxes	Fed. Income Taxes	RRSP	United Way	Total	Net pay	Chq No.	Sales Salaries Expense	Office Salaries Expense	Delivery Salaries Expense
A. Abrahams	27.00	43.00	1,161.00	40.50	1,201.50	56.14	21.99	78.20	162.40	60.08	10.00	388.80	812.70	401			1,201.50
D. Clarke	31.00	41.00	1,271.00	15.50	1,286.50	60.35	23.54	85.90	180.90	64.33	10.00	425.02	861.48	402	1,286.50		
F. Johnson	28.00	40.00	1,120.00	-	1,120.00	52.11	20.50	70.50	146.55	56.00	10.00	355.65	764.35	403		1,120.00	
M. Musson	28.00	40.00	1,120.00	-	1,120.00	52.11	20.50	70.50	146.55	56.00	25.00	370.65	749.35	404			1,120.00
L. Roberts					2,058.00	98.54	37.66	204.10	369.75	102.90	5.00	817.95	1,240.05	405	2,058.00		
C. Shultz	29.00	42.00	1,218.00	29.00	1,247.00	58.39	22.82	82.60	172.95	62.35	10.00	409.11	837.89	406		1,247.00	
I. Shroeder	30.00	38.00	1,140.00	-	1,140.00	53.10	20.86	70.50	143.95	57.00	25.00	370.41	769.59	407	1,140.00		
T. Tomison					2,610.00	125.86	47.76	302.60	511.25	130.50	25.00	1,142.98	1,467.02	408	2,610.00		
L. Vanpelt	25.00	36.00	900.00	-	900.00	41.22	16.47	43.95	86.35	45.00	15.00	247.99	652.01	409			900.00
			7,930.00	85.00	12,683.00	597.82	232.10	1,008.85	1,920.65	634.15	135.00	4,528.57	8,154.43		7,094.50	2,367.00	3,221.50

PROBLEM 10-6 ___, Concluded

.–4.

JOURNAL   PAGE

	DATE		DESCRIPTION	POST. REF.	DEBIT	CREDIT	
1							1
2							2
3							3
4							4
5							5
6							6
7							7
8							8
9							9
10							10
11							11
12							12
13							13
14							14
15							15
16							16
17							17
18							18
19							19
20							20
21							21
22							22
23							23
24							24
25							25
26							26
27							27
28							28
29							29
30							30
31							31
32							32
33							33
34							34
35							35
36							36

This page not used.

PROBLEM 10-7 ___

1.

			EARNINGS			DEDUCTIONS						Paid	Accounts Debited	
Name	Rate	Hours	Reg	OT	Gross	CPP	EI	Prov. Income Taxes	Fed. Income Taxes	RRSP	United Way	Total	Net pay	Sales Salaries Expense	Office Salaries Expense
J. Chasson															
R. Franks															
S. Ingrams															
L. Toner															
F. Ventresca															
K. Wong															

PAYROLL FOR THE WEEK ENDED April 24, 2015

PROBLEM 10-7 ___, Concluded

2–4

JOURNAL   PAGE

	DATE		DESCRIPTION	POST. REF.	DEBIT	CREDIT	
1							1
2							2
3							3
4							4
5							5
6							6
7							7
8							8
9							9
10							10
11							11
12							12
13							13
14							14
15							15
16							16
17							17
18							18
19							19
20							20

PROBLEM 10-8 ___

JOURNAL

PAGE

	DATE		DESCRIPTION	POST. REF.	DEBIT	CREDIT	
1							1
2							2
3							3
4							4
5							5
6							6
7							7
8							8
9							9
10							10
11							11
12							12
13							13
14							14
15							15
16							16
17							17
18							18
19							19
20							20
21							21
22							22
23							23
24							24
25							25
26							26
27							27
28							28
29							29
30							30
31							31
32							32
33							33
34							34
35							35
36							36

PROBLEM 10-8 ___ , Concluded

	DATE		DESCRIPTION	POST. REF.	DEBIT	CREDIT	
1							1
2							2
3							3
4							4
5							5
6							6
7							7
8							8
9							9
10							10
11							11
12							12
13							13
14							14
15							15
16							16
17							17
18							18
19							19
20							20
21							21
22							22
23							23
24							24
25							25
26							26
27							27
28							28
29							29
30							30
31							31
32							32
33							33
34							34
35							35
36							36

JOURNAL PAGE

COMPREHENSIVE PROBLEM 3

1.

JOURNAL

	DATE		DESCRIPTION	POST. REF.	DEBIT	CREDIT	
1							1
2							2
3							3
4							4
5							5
6							6
7							7
8							8
9							9
10							10
11							11
12							12
13							13
14							14
15							15
16							16
17							17
18							18
19							19
20							20
21							21
22							22
23							23
24							24
25							25
26							26
27							27
28							28
29							29
30							30
31							31
32							32
33							33
34							34
35							35
36							36

COMPREHENSIVE PROBLEM 3, Continued

1.

JOURNAL

	DATE		DESCRIPTION	POST. REF.	DEBIT	CREDIT	
1							1
2							2
3							3
4							4
5							5
6							6
7							7
8							8
9							9
10							10
11							11
12							12
13							13
14							14
15							15
16							16
17							17
18							18
19							19
20							20
21							21
22							22
23							23
24							24
25							25
26							26
27							27
28							28
29							29
30							30
31							31
32							32
33							33
34							34
35							35
36							36

COMPREHENSIVE PROBLEM 3, Continued

2.

Bank Reconciliation		

COMPREHENSIVE PROBLEM 3, Continued

3. and 4.

JOURNAL   PAGE

	DATE		DESCRIPTION	POST. REF.	DEBIT	CREDIT	
1							1
2							2
3							3
4							4
5							5
6							6
7							7
8							8
9							9
10							10
11							11
12							12
13							13
14							14
15							15
16							16
17							17
18							18
19							19
20							20
21							21
22							22
23							23
24							24
25							25
26							26
27							27
28							28
29							29
30							30
31							31
32							32
33							33
34							34
35							35
36							36

COMPREHENSIVE PROBLEM 3, Continued

JOURNAL   PAGE _____

	DATE		DESCRIPTION	POST. REF.	DEBIT	CREDIT	
1							1
2							2
3							3
4							4
5							5
6							6
7							7
8							8
9							9
10							10
11							11
12							12
13							13
14							14
15							15
16							16
17							17
18							18
19							19
20							20
21							21
22							22
23							23
24							24
25							25
26							26
27							27
28							28
29							29
30							30
31							31
32							32
33							33
34							34
35							35
36							36

COMPREHENSIVE PROBLEM 3, Continued

5.

Balance Sheet

COMPREHENSIVE PROBLEM 3, Continued

COMPREHENSIVE PROBLEM 3, Concluded

6.

PR E-1 ___

GENERAL LEDGER

1., 3., and 4.

ACCOUNT   *Cash*   ACCOUNT NO.   *1010*

DATE		ITEM	POST. REF.	DEBIT	CREDIT	BALANCE

ACCOUNT   *Accounts Receivable*   ACCOUNT NO.   *1020*

DATE		ITEM	POST. REF.	DEBIT	CREDIT	BALANCE

ACCOUNT   *Maintenance Supplies*   ACCOUNT NO.   *1040*

DATE		ITEM	POST. REF.	DEBIT	CREDIT	BALANCE

ACCOUNT   *Office Supplies*   ACCOUNT NO.   *1050*

DATE		ITEM	POST. REF.	DEBIT	CREDIT	BALANCE

PR E-1 ___ , Continued

ACCOUNT　*Office Equipment*　　ACCOUNT NO.　*1060*

DATE		ITEM	POST. REF.	DEBIT	CREDIT	BALANCE	

ACCOUNT　*Accumulated Amortization—Office Equipment*　　ACCOUNT NO.　*1070*

DATE		ITEM	POST. REF.	DEBIT	CREDIT	BALANCE	

ACCOUNT　*Vehicles*　　ACCOUNT NO.　*1080*

DATE		ITEM	POST. REF.	DEBIT	CREDIT	BALANCE	

ACCOUNT　*Accumulated Amortization—Vehicles*　　ACCOUNT NO.　*1090*

DATE		ITEM	POST. REF.	DEBIT	CREDIT	BALANCE	

PR E-1 ___ , Continued

ACCOUNT   *Accounts Payable*   ACCOUNT NO.   *2010*

DATE		ITEM	POST. REF.	DEBIT	CREDIT	BALANCE	

ACCOUNT   _____ , *Capital*   ACCOUNT NO.   *3010*

DATE		ITEM	POST. REF.	DEBIT	CREDIT	BALANCE	

ACCOUNT   _____ , *Withdrawals*   ACCOUNT NO.   *3020*

DATE		ITEM	POST. REF.	DEBIT	CREDIT	BALANCE	

ACCOUNT   *Fees Earned*   ACCOUNT NO.   *4010*

DATE		ITEM	POST. REF.	DEBIT	CREDIT	BALANCE	

PR E-1 ___ , Continued

ACCOUNT   *Rent Revenue*   ACCOUNT NO.   *4020*

DATE		ITEM	POST. REF.	DEBIT	CREDIT	BALANCE

ACCOUNT   *Driver Salaries Expense*   ACCOUNT NO.   *5010*

DATE		ITEM	POST. REF.	DEBIT	CREDIT	BALANCE

ACCOUNT   *Maintenance Supplies Expense*   ACCOUNT NO.   *5020*

DATE		ITEM	POST. REF.	DEBIT	CREDIT	BALANCE

ACCOUNT   *Fuel Expense*   ACCOUNT NO.   *5030*

DATE		ITEM	POST. REF.	DEBIT	CREDIT	BALANCE

PR E-1 ___ , Continued

ACCOUNT *Office Salaries Expense*   ACCOUNT NO. *5010*

DATE		ITEM	POST. REF.	DEBIT	CREDIT	BALANCE	

ACCOUNT *Rent Expense*   ACCOUNT NO. *5050*

DATE		ITEM	POST. REF.	DEBIT	CREDIT	BALANCE	

ACCOUNT *Advertising Expense*   ACCOUNT NO. *5060*

DATE		ITEM	POST. REF.	DEBIT	CREDIT	BALANCE	

ACCOUNT *Miscellaneous Administrative Expense*   ACCOUNT NO. *5070*

DATE		ITEM	POST. REF.	DEBIT	CREDIT	BALANCE	

PR E-1 _____, Continued

2., 3., and 4.

PURCHASES JOURNAL

PAGE 37

DATE	ACCOUNT CREDITED	POST. REF.	ACCOUNTS PAYABLE CR.	MAINTENANCE SUPPLIES DR.	OFFICE SUPPLIES DR.	OTHER ACCOUNTS DR. ACCOUNT	POST. REF.	AMOUNT	
									1
									2
									3
									4
									5
									6
									7
									8
									9
									10
									11
									12
									13
									14
									15
									16
									17
									18
									19
									20
									21
									22
									23

PR E-1 ___ , Continued

2., 3., and 4.   **CASH RECEIPTS JOURNAL**   PAGE *31*

	DATE	ACCOUNT CREDITED	POST. REF.	OTHER ACCOUNTS CR.	ACCOUNTS REC. CR.	CASH DR.	
1							1
2							2
3							3
4							4
5							5
6							6
7							7
8							8
9							9
10							10
11							11
12							12
13							13
14							14
15							15
16							16

2. and 4.   **SALES JOURNAL**   PAGE *35*

	DATE	INVOICE NO.	ACCOUNT DEBITED	POST. REF.	ACCTS. REC. DR. FEES EARNED CR.	
1						1
2						2
3						3
4						4
5						5
6						6
7						7
8						8
9						9
10						10
11						11
12						12
13						13
14						14

PR E-1 ___, Continued

2., 3., and 4.   **CASH DISBURSEMENTS JOURNAL**   PAGE *34*

	DATE	CK. NO.	ACCOUNT DEBITED	POST. REF.	OTHER ACCOUNTS DR.	ACCOUNTS PAYABLE DR.	CASH CR.	
1								1
2								2
3								3
4								4
5								5
6								6
7								7
8								8
9								9
10								10
11								11
12								12
13								13
14								14
15								15
16								16
17								17
18								18
19								19

2. and 3.   **JOURNAL**   PAGE *1*

	DATE	DESCRIPTION	POST. REF.	DEBIT	CREDIT	
1						1
2						2
3						3
4						4
5						5
6						6
7						7
8						8
9						9
10						10
11						11

PR E-1 ___ , Concluded

5.

Unadjusted Trial Balance		

6. Balance of accounts receivable control account: _____

Balance of accounts payable control account: _____

Notes